BENARES

THE SACRED CITY

BENARES

THE SACRED CITY

SKETCHES OF HINDU LIFE AND RELIGION

BY

E. B. HAVELL, A.R.C.A.

PRINCIPAL OF THE GOVERNMENT SCHOOL OF ART,
CALCUTTA

With many Illustrations

GYAN

Published by

GYAN

Gyan Publishing House
5, Ansari Road
Daryaganj, New Delhi-110002
Phone: 011-47034999, 9811692060
E-mail: books@gyanbooks.com

Distribution Network
gyanbooks.com
India, USA, Canada, UK, Australia, France

ISBN : 978-81-212-2907-4 (PB)
First Published, 1905

2nd Impression 2021

Printed at: Gyan Press, Delhi.

Benares
The Sacred City
Author: E. B. Havell

BENARES

THE SACRED CITY

SKETCHES OF HINDU LIFE AND RELIGION

BY

E. B. HAVELL, A.R.C.A.

PRINCIPAL OF THE GOVERNMENT SCHOOL OF ART, CALCUTTA

With many Illustrations

LONDON: BLACKIE & SON LIMITED
50 · OLD · BAILEY · E.C. · GLASGOW
DUBLIN · AND · BOMBAY · · MCMV

MANIKARNIKA GHÂT (page 134)

(From a photograph by Johnston & Hoffmann)

PREFACE

It is, perhaps, because Benares is not forbidden, that such a mine of human interest, and one of the most extraordinary cities of the East, is now probably less known to most Europeans than Lhasa. Even of the Europeans who have seen Benares, few have any adequate conception of the ideas and beliefs which many millions of our fellow-subjects associate with it. Few, indeed, have either the time or the inclination to read through the increasing accumulation of very solid literature which deals with the philosophic side of Hinduism; and the more popular missionary accounts (with our national tendency to underrate the enemy's strength) generally make the mistake of representing all Hinduism as a mass of degraded superstitions and idolatry, only held together by the profound ignorance and backwardness of the Indian people.

These sketches are not offered as a contribution to oriental scholarship, or to religious controversy, but as an attempt to give an intelligible outline of Hindu ideas and religious practices, and especially as a presentation of the imaginative and artistic side of Indian religions, which can be observed at few places so well as in the sacred city and its neighbourhood—the birthplace of Buddhism and of one of the principal sects of Hinduism.

The illustrations have been, for the most part, specially prepared to elucidate the text, and include some of the remarkable discoveries made this year at Sarnath. They will, it is hoped, give some idea of the wonderful artistic wealth of Benares life, and at the same time be more instructive than those of ordinary books of travel.

The authorities consulted include Sherring's *Sacred City of the Hindus*; *The Life and Times of Sri Sankaracharya*, by C. Krishnasami Aiyar; and the works of Barth, Beal, Sylvain Lévi, Rhys Davids, Monier Williams, Max Müller, Taylor, and many others. My acknowledgments are due to Messrs. E. J. Lazarus & Co., of Benares, for permission to use Mr. Ralph Griffiths' translation of the Rig-Veda; and to Messrs. Som Brothers, Calcutta, for extracts from Pandit Tattvabhushan's translations of the Upanishads.

I am indebted to H.H. the Maharajah of Benares and staff for much courteous assistance; and to Babus Abanindro Nath Tagore, Dinesh Chandra Sen, and other Indian friends for valuable information.

Mr. J. H. Marshall, Director-General of the Archæological Survey of India, Dr. Vogel, Messrs. Johnstone & Hoffman, Calcutta, and Messrs. Saeed Bros., Benares, have kindly helped me with some of the illustrations.

E. B. HAVELL.

CALCUTTA, *October, 1905.*

CONTENTS

ILLUSTRATIONS

CHAPTER I

IN THE VEDIC TIMES

History, in the conventional European sense, has never possessed much interest for the Hindu mind. Thoroughly permeated with the idea of the unreality of material things, the Brahmin priesthood, while taking extraordinary precautions to preserve their inheritance of spiritual culture, have never troubled themselves to mark the footprints which kings and dynasties leave upon the sands of time. It is chiefly through the exertions of European scholars, with the help of the old Buddhist records, that the main outlines of Indian history, previous to the Muhammadan invasions, have been made intelligible.

The detailed history of the petty kingdoms into which northern India was divided would probably possess little interest, even if it were sifted out of the wild legends which Eastern imagination has woven into it. Benares will always possess supreme interest as the chief centre of the evolution of two of the great world-religions — Brahminism and Buddhism; but while the development of Buddhism can be, to some extent, traced and mapped out with exact dates and events, the history of Brahminism must always be regarded from a different stand-point.

Of the antiquity of Benares there can hardly be any question. From its peculiar situation on the banks of a splendid river, with its eastern boundary converted by the current into a magnificent natural amphitheatre, facing the rising sun, it is not unreasonable to conjecture that even before the Aryan tribes established themselves in the Ganges valley, Benares may have been a great centre of primitive sun-worship, and that the special sanctity with which the Brahmins have invested the city is only a tradition of those primeval days, borrowed, with so many of their rites and symbols, from their Turanian predecessors.

The first definite historical event known about Benares is that the Kâsis, one of the Aryan tribes which were then occupying northern India, established themselves in the Ganges valley, near Benares, at a date supposed to be between 1400 and 1000 B.C. The origin of the Aryans is still a much-debated question, but the researches of ethnologists have completely disturbed the theory of philologists, which placed the home of the Aryan people in Central Asia, and point to more northern and western latitudes as the cradle of the race. Certainly the Aryans brought with them into India all the habits and ideas of northern people—they were fair-skinned, ate horse-flesh and beef, and drank fermented liquor—the *soma* juice, which they held to be the *amrita*, or nectar of the gods. Like the ancient Britons they were polyandrous. Their religion, at first, was a simple adoration of the beneficent powers of Nature, with little of the mysticism and dread, born of a tropical environment. They worshipped the sky,

Dyaus-pitar, as Heavenly Father, and Prithivi, the earth, as Mother; Varuna, the all-embracing firmament, the upholder of heaven and earth, king of gods and men, who made the sun and moon to shine, whose breath was the wind—

> "He knows the path of birds that fly through heaven, and sovran of the sea,
> He knows the ships that are thereon.
> True to his holy law, he knows the twelve moons with their progeny,[1]
> He knows the moon of later birth.
> He knows the pathway of the wind, the spreading-high and mighty wind.
> He knows the gods above."
>
> —*Rig-Veda, Hymn 25. Griffith's translation.*

They invoked Indra, the rain-god, as brother, friend, and father, who heard their prayers; Agni, the Fire-god, slayer of demons, who protected them day and night from evil; Surya, "the soul of all that moveth not, or moveth", and Savitri—the sun and sunshine. The early Vedic hymns are redolent with the fragrance of a bright and genial spring-time, reflecting the joy of a simple, pastoral life in the golden age, when the children of men played with Mother Nature in her kindest moods, and the earth and the stars sang together. The gloom and terrors of tropical forests, the fury of the cyclone, the scorching heat, and the mighty forces of the monsoon floods, had not yet infected Aryan life and thought. Their poets loved to sing the beauties of the dawn—Ushas, the lovely maiden, daughter of the sky; but her dark sister, Night, was also to them a kindly divinity:—

[1] The days.

"Friend of the home, the strong and youthful maiden,
Night, dear to Savitār the god, and Bhagu,
All-compassing, all-glorious, prompt to listen, hath with her greatness filled the earth and heaven.
Over all depths hath she gone up, and mounted, Most Mighty One, the sky's exalted summit.
Over me now the loving Night is spreading with her conspicuous God-like ways like Mitra.
Excellent, high-born, blissful, meet for worship, Night, thou hast come; stay here with friendly spirit.
Guard us the food for men that we have gotten, and all prosperity that comes of cattle."

—*Atharva Veda. Book xix, 49. Griffith's translation.*

They had no idols, and the nature-gods whom they worshipped provided their only temples. The Aryan ritual consisted of burnt-sacrifices, oblations of clarified butter, and libations of *soma*-juice or milk, accompanied by hymns of praise and prayer. Far back in time, in that dim region which modern historical telescopes are ever trying to explore, the father of the family was both sacrificer and priest; but when the Aryans appeared in India, their ritual had already become so complicated as to call for a separate class of priests and poets, like the Druids—the Brahmins of ancient Europe. Caste was still unknown, but the poets and thinkers of the people had already begun to concern themselves with those speculations regarding the origin of all things which form the basis of modern Hinduism:—

"There was neither existence, nor non-existence,
The kingdom of air, nor the sky beyond.

What was there to contain, to cover in—
Was it but vast, unfathomed depths of water?

There was no Death there, nor Immortality,
No sun was there, dividing day from night.

> Then was there only THAT, resting within itself.
> Apart from IT, there was not anything.
>
> At first within the darkness veiled in darkness,
> Chaos unknowable, the All lay hid,
>
> Till straightway from the formless void made manifest
> By the great power of heat was born that germ."
>
> —*Rig-Veda. Hymn of Creation.*

There had also sprung up the idea of the compelling power of prayer and sacrifice, which became the key-note of the later Brahminical ritual. Certain individuals, families, or tribes acquired a reputation for the success which followed their sacrifices and prayers, and by a *post hoc, propter hoc* line of reasoning, it was assumed that the divine powers could not only be propitiated, but coerced into granting the favours desired, whether it was victory over enemies, wealth, rain, recovery from sickness, or spiritual benefits.

The hymns and prayers which seemed specially efficacious were handed down to posterity as most precious legacies, and the rule of sacrifice gradually developed into a complicated science, the practice of which required the most exact knowledge and experience. The priestly office thus tended more and more to become a hereditary position of great power and responsibility, for though the virtue ascribed to a successful sacrifice was great, the disasters which would result from a blundering performance might involve a whole tribe or kingdom in ruin.

Every tribe had a *purohita*, or high priest, who always performed the proper sacrifices before a battle, and claimed a liberal share of the booty which might be gained from a victory. The composers of the sacred hymns, now known as the Rishis, or sages, also expected and generally received handsome rewards for their services. But some of them have celebrated the niggardliness of their patrons in sarcastic verses, which shows that their minds were not always above worldly considerations. One disappointed author, who had composed an ode to the Ashvins, the twin heralds of the dawn, and received as a reward a chariot without horses or harness, expresses his indignation thus:—

> "This teamless chariot I received from the Ashvins, owners of many horses. It gratified me greatly!
> It must get on somehow with me to the place where men drink *soma*, the precious car!
> Dreams and wealthy niggards, both are unprofitable.
> Let me have nought to do with them."

Though the *purohitas* and priests thus occupied a very important place in Aryan society, they were as yet entirely subordinate to the nobles and chiefs of the warrior class, and were very far from the position of absolute supremacy which they gained for themselves in later times. As in the middle ages in Europe, the functions of warrior and priest were often combined. Many of the finest hymns preserved in the sacred books of the Hindus were composed by the Kshatriyas, or fighting chiefs.

A very important part of the sacred lore treasured in the religious literature of the Hindus is contained in the Upanishads, the records of the debates on metaphysical questions and the theory of sacrificial practice which excited the profoundest interest of our Aryan forefathers. Kings, nobles, and priests, wise men and women, took part in the discussions. The greatest freedom of thought was allowed, and the rules which regulated the debates were only those which were approved of as likely to lead to sound conclusions. The rewards for debaters who showed profound thought and argument were not less liberal than those which were given to successful composers and sacrificers, but the penalties for those who infringed the rules of logic, or spoke foolishly, were heavy.

These disputations, or "Brahmodyams", afterwards became so much a national institution, that, if we may believe the Sanskrit traditions, even kings would yield their thrones and become the servants or pupils of the wisest philosophers. The methods of the Inquisition, and the argument of the sword and stake, never became popular with Hindu religious teachers. Whatever may be urged against the Hindu system, it must be admitted that it has always stood for absolute liberty of conscience. One religious movement after another has swept over Indian soil, but until the Muhammadan conquest it was never considered justifiable, or necessary, to suppress the voice of the preacher and the argument of the philosopher with torture, bloodshed, and judicial murder.

The old Buddhist records, though referring to a considerably later time than the Vedic period, throw much light on the character of these ancient universities, and on the distinctions which were given as rewards of learning.

A member of the Buddhist order who had thoroughly mastered one section of the philosophical books was exempted from the common drudgery of monastic duties. As he progressed the rewards were proportionately increased. When he could expound two sections he was allowed to reside in a furnished upper room. The privileges attached to expert knowledge of the third and fourth sections were the services of a number of attendants, first of a lower class, and then of lay-disciples, called "pure men", *upasakas*. For the fifth section he was granted an elephant carriage, and finally when he attained to complete knowledge of all six sections he was entitled to the dignity of an escort.

When one of the members had won all that pure scholarship could gain, and had acquired a reputation as a great teacher, he had the right to call together and preside over a meeting for philosophical discussions. In this convention he would be the judge of the merit or demerit of the debaters, commending some and reproving others. If one of them should become distinguished above the rest for elegant language, profound logic, and depth of thought, he would be placed upon a splendidly-caparisoned elephant and escorted from the convent with great state and dignity. But when a member presented an ill-reasoned argument, or tried to sustain it by breaking the rules of logic, and was feeble and clumsy in his rhetoric, the assembly would paint his face, smear him with dirt, and then take him from the monastery to some deserted place, or throw him in a ditch. "Thus they distinguish between worth and demerit, between the wise and the foolish."

The natural evolution of Aryan thought and religion had so far produced three classes of literature—first the Vedic hymns, which I have already described; secondly the Brahmanas, which embody the priestly traditions of sacrifice; and thirdly the Upanishads, or philosophical discussions. Sanskrit scholars have made widely different estimates of the periods covered by these three classes. No doubt the hymns of the Vedas reflect traditions of the Aryans long antecedent to the time when they reached India. Max Müller has fixed the date to which they belong as approximately B.C. 2000; other authorities place them as far back as B.C. 6000; while an Indian scholar, Mr. Tilak, from a study of the astronomical data given by the Rig-Veda, and from the description of the dawn and sunrise, and the phenomena of the seasons, believes that some of them refer to a time when the original Aryan home must have been at or near the Arctic circle.

The Brahmanas probably represent a development of Hinduism, for the most part, if not entirely, Indian. The age of their first compilation has been put between B.C. 1300 and B.C. 1100, but there are many later additions extending to perhaps B.C. 600. They are an extraordinary compilation of ritual practice and explanation, evolved by the imaginations of the priestly families, who piled form upon form and rite upon rite, until the simple piety of the early Aryans was buried in a mass of superstitious observances.

To European readers they are chiefly interesting for the light they throw upon modern Hindu ritual, and for the Aryan legends regarding the creation and the flood which have been preserved in them. The story of the deluge is as follows:—

The seventh Manu of the fourteen mythical progenitors of mankind was one day washing his hands when he caught a fish. The fish spoke and said,

"Take care of me, and protect me from the big fish that would eat me, and I will one day save you". Manu asked, "From what will you save me?" The fish answered, "A flood will come and destroy all living creatures. I will save you from that." Manu kept the fish in a jar, until it grew so big that it begged to be put into a ditch, at the same time telling Manu to build a ship to prepare for the coming catastrophe. Manu built the ship accordingly, and as the fish grew too big for the ditch, carried it down to the sea. When the flood came, Manu tied the ship to the horn of the fish, which dragged him swiftly towards the northern mountains, the Himalayas. Arrived there, the fish instructed him to tie his ship to the mountain-top, and then swam away.

As the flood subsided, the ship gradually descended the slope of the mountain, and Manu left it to perform worship and sacrifices. After a year a woman was produced from the sacrifices. Manu asked, "Who art thou?" "Thy daughter," she replied. "How, illustrious one, art thou my daughter?" he asked. She answered, "Those offerings of ghee, sour milk, whey and curds, which thou madest in the waters, with them thou hast begotten me. I am the blessing; make use of me at the sacrifice! If thou wilt do so, thou wilt become rich in offspring and cattle." He accordingly made use of her as the benediction in the middle of the sacrifice. "With her he went on worshipping and toiling in religious rites, wishing for offspring. Through her he generated this race, which is the race of Manu."

The Upanishads, like the Brahmanas, are now incorporated in the four Vedas. Their first compilation is attributed to a time shortly after the offshoots from the first Aryan settlement of the Punjab began to spread to the Ganges valley. They form the basis of the later schools of Indian philosophy. Though deeply tinged with Oriental mysticism, they, unlike the Brahmanas, are almost free from ritualism and sectarian spirit; they are chiefly devoted to discussions as to the nature and means of realizing a knowledge of Brahman, the Universal Soul and Cause of all things.

The Brahmanas and Upanishads, in fact, seem to represent two different currents of thought, which can be traced throughout the whole development of Hinduism. The one, the exclusiveness and pedantry of the narrow-minded priest, always concerned with the interests of priestcraft; the other, the true religious feelings of the people, interpreted by their most earnest thinkers.

The ethical stand-point of the Aryan race, as put forward in the Upanishads some three thousand years ago, can hardly be surpassed in the present day:—

"Having taught him the Vedas, a teacher exhorts his pupils thus: 'Speak the truth. Practise virtue. Do not neglect the study of the Vedas. Having paid the honorarium to your preceptor (*i.e.* having returned home at the close of your studies), do not cut off the line of children (*i.e.* marry and bring up a family). Do not swerve from the truth. Do not swerve from virtue. Do not swerve from the good. Do not be indifferent to the attainment of greatness. Do not neglect your duties to the gods and to your parents. Honour your mother as a deity. Honour your father as a deity. Honour your guest as a deity. Do those deeds which are commendable, and not those that are otherwise. Imitate our good deeds, and not those that are otherwise. . . . Give alms with a willing heart. Do not give with an unwilling heart. Give wisely. Give with modesty. Give with fear. Give with a sympathetic heart.'"[1]

The story of Yama and Nachiketâ is the most characteristic in the Upanishads. It is as follows:—

Nachiketâ was a young Brahmin, who, having been hastily vowed by his father as a victim to Yama, the god of Death, cheerfully submitted, even though his father repented of his vow and hesitated to fulfil it. Owing to Death's absence when Nachiketâ arrived at his abode, he remained three nights without food. On his return Yama, as an apology for the slight to his Brahmin guest, begged of him to ask for any three boons he might desire.

Nachiketâ's first request was that his father might have peace of mind and cease to feel anger towards him. This was immediately granted. The next was that Death would explain to him the manner of producing the sacrificial fire which led to heaven. To this also Death readily assented. Nachiketâ's last boon was that Death would tell him what all men desired to know, the mystery of the future life.

Yama said: "Ask for sons and grandsons who shall live a hundred years; ask for wealth, pleasure, power, long life for yourself—all that men hold most precious, but only not this—ask me no question about death".

Nachiketâ replied: "In all these things you offer, O Death, no wise man will take delight. They are things of a day; even all life is short. Keep your

[1] The Upanishads. Translated by Sitanath Tattvabhusan. Som Brothers, 1904. Vol. II. p. 104.

pleasures, power, and riches. The boon I have asked I have asked."

Then Yama said: "The good, the pleasant, these are separate things, with different objects, binding all mankind. They who accept the good, alone are wise. They who prefer the pleasant, miss life's real aim.

"Fools who live in darkness, believing themselves wise and learned, wander in devious ways, like blind men led by blind.

"To the man without understanding, thoughtless and deceived by wealth, the future life is not revealed. He who thinks this world alone exists, and the future is not, must yield himself to me time after time.

"The knowledge you would gain cannot be gained by reasoning. Few have the means of hearing it, few after hearing can understand it. It is subtler than an atom, and beyond the ken of reason.

"The wise man who has realized by spiritual communion that Divine Being,[1] invisible, hidden, pervading all things, who is in the heart and lives in inaccessible places, gives up both joy and sorrow."

Nachiketâ said: "That which is different from virtue and different from vice, different from the chain of cause and effect, different from the past and future, tell me of that":

Yama replied: "The Worshipful One, whom all the Vedas tell of, to whom all discipline of mind and body is directed, for whom men acquire spiritual knowledge, I will speak to you briefly of that Worshipful One. He is AUM.

"Verily this syllable is Brahman, this syllable is the Highest. Knowing this, one obtains every desire.

[1] Brahman, the Universal Soul, or Self.

"This help is the best, this help is the highest. Knowing this, one becomes glorified in the world of Brahman.

"The real Self is neither born, nor dies. It is not produced, nor is aught produced from it. It is unborn, eternal, everlasting, and ancient. When the body is destroyed, it is not destroyed.

"If the slayer thinks he slays the Self, and if the slain believes the Self is slain, both are ignorant. The Self is neither slain nor slays.

"The wise man knowing the Self to be incorporeal—though existing in changing bodies—knowing it great and all-pervading, is free from grief.

"This Self cannot be realized by the Vedas, nor by reason, nor by learning. The wicked cannot know it, nor he whose mind is not at rest. It manifests itself to itself. Only Self knows Self."[1]

We may picture Benares in the later Vedic times as one of the first Aryan settlements in the Ganges valley—a clearing in the primeval forest, perhaps first occupied by the Dravidians or Kolarians. There they kept their cattle and cultivated the soil with the help of the conquered aboriginals, whom they called Dasyus. Their ordinary dwellings were probably of mud, roofed with bamboos and thatch—very like those in the villages round Benares now; the better ones might have been partly of brick or stone, plastered over and decorated with paintings in fresco, the most ancient form of pictorial art, such as the oldest Buddhist records describe.

It was an admirable site for such a settlement. The rich alluvial soil afforded plenty of sustenance for men

[1] Abridged from Pandit Tattvabhusan's translation.

and cattle. The Ganges was at the same time a protection from hostile invasions, and an easy highway of communication with the older Aryan settlements in the Punjab. The river Barna on the north, and the Asi on the south—a more important stream than it is now—gave protection from sudden attacks of the fierce aboriginal tribes dwelling in the densest forests, and called by the Aryans Rakshasas, demons. It only needed a wall or forts on the west to make the little colony secure on all sides.

The cool bathing in the splendid river and worship on its sunny banks would afford to the Aryan settlers refreshment for body and soul. So even in those remote times the place may have acquired a reputation as being propitious for the favoured people, and thus to them sacred soil, an oasis of spiritual life in the midst of the impious non-Aryan tribes, like Brahmâvarta, their much-beloved home in the north-west.

It has been supposed that the spiritual leaders of the Aryans began, about the time when the Kâsis first appeared in the Ganges valley, to arrange the compilation of the Vedic hymns, the Brahmanas and the Upanishads, in order to preserve their traditional faith from the risk of corruption which was incurred by intermarriage with the Dravidian and Kolarian neighbours. Benares, therefore, may perhaps have begun already to establish its reputation as a great seat of Aryan philosophy and religion.

The first idea of caste, which was mainly that of race protection, originated at the same period, and from the same cause. But caste as it is now understood did not become a fixed institution for many centuries later. Even in the sixth century B.C., though there were restrictions as to eating together, and a fair complexion was regarded as indicating high birth, a low occupation by itself did not involve any social ostracism. A Brahmin or Kshatriya could work at a trade or engage in agriculture without any dishonour or penalty.

CHAPTER II

THE HINDU EPICS—HERO-WORSHIP

In order to follow the further development of Hindu religion and society from the time the Kâsis established themselves in the valley of the Ganges, it is necessary to understand the political situation which confronted the Aryan settlers in northern India. They were by no means a united people, but composed of numerous tribes and clans, not all of pure Aryan stock, often fighting with each other, and surrounded not only by savage aboriginals of the lowest type living in the dense forests, and classed by the Aryans as Rakshasas, or demons, but by a medley of other races in various stages of civilization and with all manner of religious beliefs. The Dravidians, who, like the Aryans, had entered India from the north-west, were probably more advanced in the industrial arts, and had developed into petty kingdoms, with many of which the Aryans formed alliances, both in the fighting which resulted from tribal disputes, and in their foreign wars.

There were two political parties in the Aryan camp: one headed by Vasishtha, a Rishi of the priestly caste, who represented the school of orthodoxy and exclusiveness; and the other by Vishwâmitra, a Kshatriya, or warrior chief, who became the leader and spiritual adviser of one of the larger non-Aryan tribes which adopted the Aryan religious teaching. The Aryans themselves were a mere handful amidst a multitude, and Vishwâmitra probably realized the danger of a wholly aggressive and exclusive policy. For a long time, however, pride of race kept most of the Aryans aloof from their dark-skinned neighbours, and Brahmâvarta, "that land created by the gods, which lies between the two divine rivers Saraswatî and Drishadwatî",[1] or the part of the Punjab which they first occupied, was held to be the only soil fit for the faithful people.

But as fresh immigrations pressed in upon the original settlers, and the more enterprising of the clans pushed farther south and east, more of the so-called Turanian races were admitted into the Aryan fold, and there gradually accumulated round the pure Aryan doctrines a vast agglomeration of the primitive native faiths and purely Indian traditions which constitute the basis of the popular Hinduism of to-day. The caste system which was evolved out of these peculiar political and social conditions provided, on the one hand, an automatic system of subdivision to make room for social development and differences of religious practice; and, on the other hand, for the consolidation of all the heterogeneous elements of which Hinduism is composed into one great community of beliefs, impelled by common sentiments which bring every sect and caste and grade of society to worship together on the banks of the Ganges. The effect of this continual process of subdivision may be realized from the fact that, whereas Manu, the Hindu Moses, legislated for four castes only, Brahmins, Kshatriyas, Vaisyas, and

[1] Manu, II. 17.

Sudras, the Brahmins alone are now made up of over a hundred castes, each with different customs, and neither intermarrying nor eating together.

Though it may be urged that the caste system has helped to perpetuate many gross superstitions and revolting customs, it was nevertheless admirably adapted for the purpose of preventing Aryan culture and civilization from being entirely swallowed up in the whirlpool of contending races which confronted them in the early period of their development. The Aryan race, indeed, has been so modified by its Indian environment that probably the pure Aryan stock no longer exists, but Aryan culture and Aryan philosophy form the cement which now binds Hindu society together from one end of India to the other.

The means by which the Aryans handed down to posterity their great storehouse of spiritual wisdom, learning, and science, together with their national epics and social regulations, were not the least remarkable of their political ideas. For many centuries after Sanskrit had ceased to be spoken by the people, and a written language had come into common use, the ever-increasing accumulations of Sanskrit learning were preserved by an extraordinary system of memorizing, aided by elaborate and most scientific methods of grammar and etymology, which extended to the counting of each verse, word, and syllable, and took note of the pronunciation, accent, and intonation of the sacred texts.

The most stringent laws were enacted to prevent the Vedas from being corrupted by common use. Manu says, "He who acquires without permission the Veda from one who recites it, incurs the guilt of stealing the Veda, and shall sink into hell" (II. 116). Gautama, the reputed author of another set of regulations, lays down that "the ears of a Sudra who listens intentionally when the Veda is being recited are to be filled with molten lead. His tongue is to be cut out if he recite it. His body is to be split in twain if he preserve it in his memory." On the other hand, the Brahmin who forgot the sacred writings or divulged them to unauthorized persons was subject to various penances.

Though the earliest Sanskrit records date back to thousands of years before Christ, the first known manuscripts are not much earlier than the sixteenth century of our era. The great epics, the Mahâbhârata and the Râmâyana, and sacred books like the Bhagavat Gîta, have long ago been translated into the vernaculars. The celebrated Hindi translation of the Râmâyana is said to have been written by Tulsi Dâs in the neighbourhood of Benares, about 1574 A.D. But learned Brahmins are still to be seen at Benares, especially during the great Hindu festivals, swaying to and fro on the carved chair of a Vyas, or public reader, as they recite the sonorous Sanskrit *slokas* and translate a Vedic story, or expound what the vulgar are permitted to know of the ancient wisdom, to crowds of intent listeners.

One cannot be in Benares city many hours without noticing how closely the stories of the Râmâyana and Mahâbhârata are interwoven with Hindu thoughts and fancies. The pilgrims who pass in the boats on the river chant one refrain—Râm! Râm! Sîtâ-Râm! It is echoed by the ash-besmeared *Sadhus* along the ghats, and scrawled by school-boys on the walls. Râma

A VYAS, OR PUBLIC READER, AT BENARES

(From a photograph by Johnston & Hoffmann)

and Sîtâ, Hanuman the king of monkeys, Krishna and the great fights of the Mahâbhârata are the subject of innumerable paintings on the walls of temples, monasteries, and houses. Huge sprawling figures of Bhîma with his club are modelled in the river mud. The five Pândava brothers are worshipped in temples both in the city and along the Panch-kôsi road.

The main story of the Mahâbhârata is an account of the great war between the Aryan tribes of northern India, called the Bharatas, assisted by their Dravidian or Kolarian allies, which is supposed to have taken place between 1400 and 1300 B.C. The heroes on one side are the five Pândava princes, sons of Pându, king of Hastinapur, whose names were Yudhishthira, Bhîma, and Arjuna by one wife, and Nakula and Sahadeva by another. They were assisted by Krishna, whose worship as one of the incarnations of Vishnu is the chief popular cult of modern Hinduism. After his children were born, Pându took the vow of an ascetic, and retired into the forest, leaving the government of his kingdom to his blind brother, Dhritarâshtra, and Bhishma, his uncle.

The opponents of the Pândavas were the hundred sons of Dhritarâshtra, known as the Kuru princes, or Kauravas. The eldest, Duryodhana, who claimed the succession to the throne, was mean, spiteful, and cruel, while the Pândavas and Draupadi, "loveliest of women", who was their common wife, were types of chivalry, honour, and virtue. The chief heroes on the Kauravas' side were their uncle, Bhishma, who vainly endeavoured to reconcile the contending parties, and Karna, a half-brother of the Pândavas, who was probably of Dravidian descent. Arjuna and Karna are the Achilles and Hector of this Indian Iliad. The quarrel finally ended in a Homeric struggle, lasting for eighteen days, on the field of Kurukshetra, outside the modern Delhi. In the terrific slaughter which took place all the Kurus were annihilated, and only seven of the Pându army, including the five brothers, were left. Yudhishthira was then crowned king at Hastinapur.

The climax is the renunciation of the kingdom by all the five brothers, and their journey together towards Indra's heaven, on Mount Meru, beyond the Himalayas. But, except Yudhishthira, none could shake themselves entirely free from worldly attachments, and one by one they perished on the way, until the sole survivor, and a faithful dog which followed him, were met by Indra at the gates of heaven. After further tests of his constancy, in which Yudhishthira refused to part with his dog, and went to seek for the souls of his wife and brothers in the regions of hell, all the Pândavas were at last reunited in Indra's abode of eternal peace.

Around the original story there have accumulated in the course of many centuries a number of beautiful legends—such as that of Savitri, the devoted wife who by her insistence released her husband's spirit from the hands of Death—moral discourses, and religious treatises, including the famous Bhagavat Gíta, which is virtually the Hindu Bible of the present day. The Mahâbhârata, as it now stands, contains in poetic form a moral and religious code which is part and parcel of Hindu practice and belief.

The Râmâyana refers to a later period, supposed to be about 1000 B.C., when the Kosalas, another branch of the Aryan family which claimed descent from the sun, had pushed down to the present Oudh and north Behar, and established there a great city, Ayodhya, which is described as the centre of Aryan culture and religion. The Kâsis, as before mentioned, were at this time in the district of Benares. While the Mahâbhârata stirs the imagination with tales of mighty warriors and political strife, the Râmâyana is pervaded with tender sentiments of domestic virtue and affection, tried by many sufferings and misfortunes.

The first part describes the boyhood and youth of Râma, son of Dasaratha, king of Ayodhya, by his first queen, Kausalyâ, and heir-apparent; his exploits at the tournament, where he breaks the famous bow of Shiva and wins for his bride the fair Sîtâ, daughter of Janaka, king of the Videhas. She was miraculously born of a field-furrow. Dasaratha was about to resign the throne in favour of Râma, when an intrigue of the Queen Kaikeyî inveigles him into naming Bharat, his younger son by Kaikeyî, as his heir, and a decree of fourteen years' banishment against the elder.

Râma and Sîtâ, accompanied by Lakshman, another half-brother, then wander into the forests of Central India and take refuge with a holy hermit, called Valmiki, the reputed author of the poem. Dasaratha shortly afterwards dies of grief. Bharat, who had refused to accept the regency to which he was not justly entitled, followed Râma to his retreat, and having endeavoured, without success, to persuade him to come back, returned himself to Ayodhya with Râma's sandals to place on the throne as a symbol of the rightful king's authority. The three exiles then wander farther south beyond the Vindhya mountains to a hermitage on the banks of the Godavari, where another famous Rishi dwelt. There they lived in a hut the faithful Lakshman had built of bamboos and branches of trees, enjoying the peace and beauty of the primeval forest and performing the holy rites of their religion.

> "And they prayed to gods and fathers with each rite and duty done,
> And they sang the ancient *mantra* to the red and rising sun."[1]

Their happiness was soon, however, rudely disturbed by the abduction of Sitâ by Râvana, the king of the demons, who appeared before her in the disguise of an anchorite, while Râma and Lakshman were absent, and carried her through the air on his magic car to his royal palace in Ceylon. The rest of the story describes Sitâ's despair and sufferings in the demon king's palace, the wanderings of Râma and Lakshman in search of her, and the discovery of her by the help of Hanuman, the monkey king of the Nilgiri mountains. With Hanuman and his monkey troops Râma attacks and kills Râvana and his demon chieftains, and takes his stronghold by storm. Finally the exiles, accompanied by Hanuman, return to Ayodhya on the magic car taken from Râvana, and Râma and Sitâ are crowned amidst the rejoicings of gods and men.

A sequel, of later date than the original story, gives a sad ending to the Râmâyana. Some slanderous tongues in Ayodhya began to whisper suggestions regarding Sitâ's conduct while in the palace of Râvana, and Râma's jealousy was aroused by finding

[1] R. C. Dutt's abridged translation of the Râmâyana.

THE CORONATION OF RÂMA AND SÎTÂ

(From an old Indian picture)

a drawing of Râvana which Sîtâ had scrawled on the floor while conversing with her handmaids about her captivity. Sîtâ was banished to the forest, where she gave birth to two sons, Lava and Kusha, who were brought up by the hermit Valmiki. They were recognized by Hanuman as the sons of Râma. According to one version, Sitâ and her sons then returned to Ayodhya and passed the rest of her days in happiness with her husband; but another story is that the boys wandered into Ayodhya accidentally, and were recognized and acknowledged by Râma, who sent for Sîtâ, and in public assembly called upon her to attest her innocence.

Sîtâ in an agonized appeal invokes her Mother Earth to come to her aid and be witness of her purity.

> "Then the earth was rent and parted, and a golden throne arose;
> Held aloft by jewelled Nâgas as the leaves enfold the rose,
> And the mother in embraces held her spotless, sinless child."

Sîtâ sank back into the earth, and Râma in despair sacrificed himself in the river Sarayu.

Mr. Romesh Chandra Dutt, whose abridged English translation I have quoted, says of the Mahâbhârata and Râmâyana: "It is not an exaggeration to say that the two hundred millions of Hindus of the present day cherish in their hearts the story of their ancient epics. The Hindu scarcely lives, man or woman, high and low, educated or ignorant, whose earliest recollections do not cling round the story and the characters of the great epics. An almost illiterate oil-manufacturer of Bengal spells out some modern translation of the Mahâbhârata to while away his leisure hour. The tall and stalwart peasantry of the north-west know of the five Pandav brothers and of their friend the righteous Krishna. . . . The morals inculcated in these tales sink into the hearts of a naturally religious people, and form the basis of their moral education."

The sentiment of hero-worship is still as strong in the Hindu mind as it was three thousand years ago, and the philosophy of Hinduism finds nothing unreasonable in according divine honours to a man, woman, or child, alive or dead, who is considered to have manifested in some special sense the nature of the supreme soul which is believed to be a part of every individual.

The extremes to which this doctrine can be pushed by Hindus of the present day is described by Mr. H. H. Risley in the report of the last census:—

"Priests and priestesses, pious ascetics and successful dacoits, Indian soldiers of fortune and British men of action, bridegrooms who met their death on their wedding-day and virgins who died unwed, jostle each other in a fantastic Walpurgis dance, where new performers are constantly joining and old ones seldom go out. . . .

"In 1884 Keshub Chandra Sen, the leader of the Brahmo Somaj, narrowly escaped something closely resembling deification at the hands of a section of his disciples. A revelation was said to have been received enjoining that the chair used by him during his life should be set apart and kept sacred, and the legal member of the Viceroy's council was invited to arbitrate in the matter. Sir Courtenay Ilbert discreetly refused 'to deal with testimony of a kind inadmissible in a court of justice'. . . . Sivaji, the founder of the

Mahratta confederacy, has a temple and image in one of the bastions of the fort at Malvan in the Ratnagiri district, and is worshipped by the caste of fishermen. This seems to be a local cult imperfectly developed, as there are no priests and no regular ritual. . . . Portraits of Yashvantrao, a subordinate revenue officer in Khandesh, who ruined himself by promiscuous alms-giving and sacrificed his official position to his reluctance to refuse the most impossible requests, are worshipped to-day by thousands of devout householders. Far down in the south of India I have come across cheap lithographs of a nameless Bombay ascetic, the Swami of Akalkot in Sholapur, who died about twenty years ago. In life the Swami seems to have been an irritable saint, for he is said to have pelted with stones any ill-advised person who asked questions about his name and antecedents. As he was reported to be a Mutiny refugee, he may have had substantial reasons for guarding his incognito. He is now revered from the Deccan to Cape Comorin as Dattatreya, a sort of composite incarnation of Brahmâ, Vishnu, and Shiva, and has a temple and monastery of his own."

It should be stated, however, that the original Dattatreya, who has gained so much veneration, is not the Swami of Akalkot, but a much older saint, or previous incarnation, who is said to have been a son of one of the Vedic Rishis.

CHAPTER III

THE ADVENT OF BUDDHA—SARNATH AND THE LATEST DISCOVERIES—THE JAINS

We have brought down the development of modern Hinduism to the time when the great epics began to assume their present shape, and when speculation as to the future life and the origin of the soul had culminated in the philosophy of the Upanishads. We now arrive at the time, which may be fixed roughly from 800 to 500 B.C., when we begin to get on firmer historical ground, and approach to the great parting of the ways which came with the advent of Buddha. It is necessary to explain briefly the differences which led to the breach between Buddha and the orthodox teaching of his day. In the basis of his philosophic teaching Buddha was a Hindu of the Hindus. The Brahmins of his time taught the whole theory of the transmigration of souls; Buddha's doctrine was but a slight modification of it. They held that human suffering was to be destroyed by the termination of the cycle of re-births; Buddha taught practically the same. The main point of difference between the two was, that whereas the Brahmanas, which contain the essence of the sacerdotal doctrine, declare that "sacrifice in its totality is the bark which carries one to heaven", and that the Brahminical teaching is the only means of salvation, Buddha denied the divine authority of the Vedas, rejected the theory of sacrifice, and declared that the Eight-fold Path was the way by which all suffering was annihilated, through right views, right resolve, right speech, right actions and living, right effort, right self-knowledge, and right meditation.

To realize the revolution which Buddha effected in the whole development of Hinduism, it is necessary to understand something of the tyranny of rites and penances, with which the priestly class had then enveloped the spiritual teaching of the people. The original process of Vedic sacrifice was based on the theory that gods and men shared between them the ordering of the universe, and that the one party was bound to assist the other. If no rain fell on the earth, it was because the gods needed refreshment. They were refreshed with Soma, the nectar of the gods, and with milk from the earthly cows, which had their counterpart in the heavenly cattle—the clouds of the sky. The god Agni — Fire and Light—was brought down to the earth by the friction of two sticks, and refreshed with oblations of clarified butter (ghee), which he licked up with his seven tongues. The gods came down from heaven to attend the sacrifices, and took their seats on the place spread with the sacred *kusha* grass. The Brahmanas declare that formerly the gods and men on one side, and the *pitris*, ancestors of men, on the other, sat and feasted there together. At one time the gods and *pitris* were visible; they still are present, but invisible. "The gods subsist on what we offer them here below, just as men subsist on the gifts which come from heaven." As nourishment for the gods, and as thank-offerings for favours received, men must give presents of what they valued most, both to the gods themselves and to the priests whose knowledge of the sacred lore brought the gods to earth.

The presents to the gods were the victims which were sacrificed. The Aryans at some very remote period of their history offered human victims, the first-born of the family, as the supreme sacrifice. The horse was next in value, and after that the cow. As the science of the Aryan ritual became more developed, it was not considered necessary to actually sacrifice the victims. They were formally offered and then released. The Brahmanas describe the gradual development of a more humane ritual as follows:—"The gods, at the beginning, sacrificed man as victim; when he was sacrificed, the sacrificial virtue which was in him left him. It entered into the horse. They sacrificed a horse; when it was sacrificed, the sacrificial virtue left it and entered into a cow. When the cow was sacrificed, the sacrificial virtue which it had left it and entered into a sheep. When the sheep was sacrificed, the sacrificial virtue which it had left it and entered into a goat. The sacrificial virtue has remained in the goat the longest." The goat is the victim now most frequently offered to Durgâ and Kâlî.

Another passage in the Brahmanas describes how the sacrificial virtue passed from the goat into the earth. The gods dug in the earth to get it, and found it in rice and barley. This is the explanation given for the oblations of rice and barley now made to Shiva the Destroyer.

The essential accompaniments to the sacrifices were,

first, suitable prayers, the correct composition of which was a matter of vital importance. The gods did not enter into communication with everybody, but only with a Brahmin, a Kshatriya, or a Vaisya.[1] The next were the presents to the priests. These gave the sacrifice the force which carried it to the abode of the gods. The value of the presents was regulated by the importance of the sacrifice, and the scale for the more important sacrifices was so high that none but the richest could undertake them. The third essential was faith in the efficacy of the sacrifice.

The nature of these sacrificial rites had gradually been corrupted from the simple Aryan forms of offerings and prayers into a science of divine magic, practised both by gods and men, through which it was believed that the whole creation originated, and the whole universe was controlled. The gods had become gods through sacrifice, and men were also capable of becoming immortal if they acquired sufficient knowledge of the sacred wisdom. To protect their dominions from the invasions of men, the gods concluded a bargain with Death that no man should become immortal without first surrendering his body to him. They were constantly watching to introduce errors into the sacrifices performed on earth. Hence the necessity for extreme care and attention to every detail. Finally, sacrifice itself became a god, and the greatest of all gods.

The recitation and chanting of the hymns or *mantras*, which accompanied and formed part of the sacrifices, was no less abstruse and complicated a science than the sacrifice proper. The Vedic hymns were first

[1] The three highest classes, afterwards castes.

arranged in a series according to metre, which had a mystic significance and power in each of the three worlds, the earth, the atmosphere, and the abode of the gods. The Brahmanas compare the imaginary journey of the sacrifice and sacrificer to the heavenly regions to an earthly journey which the traveller makes by stages, taking fresh horses and oxen at each stage. In the same way the sacrificer must use fresh metres at every stage of the sacrifice to carry him on his journey heavenwards. The number of verses used together, the accent and intonation, all had a share in the efficacy of the rites.

A form of recitation is given in the Aitareya Brahmana which is called the rite of dûrohana, or the ascent into heaven. "After the invocation, the ascent of dûrohana is made. At first the reciter makes a pause at every quarter-verse. He thus starts from this world. Then he makes a pause at every half-verse; by this means he reaches the atmosphere. Then he makes a pause at every three-quarters of a verse. He arrives now in the celestial regions. By then reciting the whole verse without pausing he arrives in the solar world which shines up above." The priest now reverses the order of recitation, and brings the sacrificer back to earth, "just as one who seizes the bough of a tree". If the sacrificer, however, prefers to remain in the solar world after his arrival there, the priest omits the last part of the rite, but the sacrificer is sure to die soon afterwards.[1] The solar world, according to Hindu theories, is the abode of spirits who have completed their earthly incarnations.

[1] Ait. xviii. 7.

As the ultimate aim was to render humanity immortal, and the sacrificial science was based on an imaginary science of the celestial world, everything abnormal, weird, and uncanny was believed to have a special virtue. Everything human and normal was opposed to the success of the sacrifice. The opposition between the terrestrial sphere and the heavenly world was so pronounced that "no" for the gods was "aye" for men. Even at the present day many common Indian customs and practices are exactly the reverse of those in Europe.

The complication of the Brahminical rites became almost inconceivable. The great Horse-sacrifice, generally undertaken only by kings, especially to procure offspring, was said to conquer all sin, to render the sacrificer invulnerable and certain of victory over his enemies; but the risk of errors creeping in must have deterred many from attempting it, for it was a ceremony which took several years to complete, required the attendance of hundreds of priests and attendants, the recitation of thousands of prayers and *mantras*, endless rites, and the most lavish presents. The blessings to be gained and the evils to be avoided by the performance of appropriate rites were both material and spiritual. The Brahmanas provide the necessary *mantras* for destroying Rakshasas (demons), or human enemies, for the removal of sin, to recover lost property or to bring success to the gambler, and to avert the evil influence of an animal sitting down, trembling, or running away at the time of the sacrifice.

Closely allied to the sacrificial system was the practice of bodily penances, or mortification of the flesh, which the Brahmins regarded as a sure way, leading to immortality, and infinite worldly advantages both in this life and in the next. The Mahâbhârata mentions a princess of Benares who practised fearful penances in order to revenge herself on Bhishma, and at last threw herself into the sacrificial fire so that she might kill him in a future existence. It also relates a story of two brothers of the race of Asuras, evil spirits, enemies of the gods, who, in order to conquer the three worlds, earth, air, and heaven, underwent frightful austerities; standing for years on their toes, with arms uplifted and eyes fixed, and throwing pieces of their own flesh into the sacrificial fire. The gods were alarmed at the powers they were thus accumulating, and tried to interfere, without success. Brahmâ, the Creator, finally appeared before them, and though he refused to grant them immortality because they had undergone the penances only from the desire of sovereignty — an unworthy motive which detracted from the merit of their penances—he was constrained to allow that they should be incapable of being killed by any other being in the universe. They forthwith proceeded to make war on the region of Indra, and vanquished the Rakshasas and every creature ranging the sky. Next they slew the Nâgas, the inmates of the ocean, and all the tribes of the Mlechchas.[1] Finally, they slaughtered the Brahmins, destroyed their sacrifices, and desolated the earth. Brahmâ then interfered. With the help of Vishvakarma, the heavenly artificer, he created a damsel, whose surpassing charms not even gods could resist. She was sent to the two brothers, who, in a violent quarrel over her, killed one another, much to the relief of the distracted universe.

[1] Foreigners, barbarians.

It was when this dismal obscurantism and thaumaturgic priestcraft seemed likely to infect the whole religious thought of the people, that a new teacher came to bring back the spirituality of the ancient Vedic faith into the Aryan religion. It must not be supposed, however, that Buddha was the first to question the authority of the priesthood and to dispute the efficacy of sacrifices and penances. The hereditary priestly families had not yet established a monopoly or undisputed leadership in religious thought. The Kshatriyas, or warrior class, still stood at the head of Aryan society, and were by no means disposed to accept the Brahmins as their superiors in spiritual knowledge. Even among the Brahmins there were many who did not follow the orthodox priestly doctrines. There were, besides, a numerous class of Bhiksus, or religious devotees, both men and women, who though living an ascetic life as wandering mendicants, yet performed no sacrifices nor practised penances. These were the forerunners of the *Sadhus*, *byragis*, or fakirs of the present day. There were thus already many schools of thought outside the orthodox priestly families when Buddha's magnetic genius came to shape their somewhat nebulous theories with a new philosophy and rule of life.

About the year B.C. 557 Siddartha Gautama, son of the chief of the Sakya clan, was born in Kapilavastu, the capital of a petty state in the Nepal Terai. The story of his early life and of the Great Renunciation, when he left his wife and child and his father's palace to adopt a religious life as a Bhiksu, is too familiar to need repetition. He first attached himself to two Brahmin teachers, who taught him the theories of

Hindu philosophy commonly accepted. Finding no satisfaction in these, he wandered farther, and spent six weary years with five disciples in the forests near the Vindhyan mountains, practising the system of self-torture and starvation which the orthodox school regarded as the road to immortality.

Still dissatisfied, he again resumed the ordinary life of a Bhiksu, whereupon his disciples left him in disgust and went to Benares. He himself wandered on to the neighbourhood of the present Buddh Gaya. Then there followed, under the shade of the sacred pippal tree, known hereafter as the tree of wisdom, the short period of terrible mental agony which Indian poets and artists have pictured as his struggle with the Prince of Evil, Mara, and the wiles of his voluptuous daughters. Everything he had abandoned of worldly comfort and delight, his home, a loving wife and child, wealth, power, and pleasure, seemed to beckon to him to return. But his spiritual nature triumphed at last, and he arose, with convictions formed and mind at rest, to preach those cheerful doctrines of love and contentment which changed the entire current of Eastern thought.

Having thus become the Buddha—the Enlightened—he started off to Benares "to establish the kingdom of righteousness, to give light to those enshrouded in darkness, and to open the gates of immortality to men". He rejoined his old disciples in a deer-park, an enclosure where deer were protected from hunters, and a favourite retreat for religious devotees, at Isapattana, the modern Sarnath, 3½ miles to the north of Benares. He first preached to them the fundamental principles of his doctrines: the uselessness of bodily penances—

misery was a necessary accompaniment of existence —men needed no priests nor sacrifices to help them to escape from the cycle of transmigrations—the means lay in their own hearts, through the destruction of evil desires, worldliness, doubt, ignorance, and vexation.

At the time when Buddha began his preaching, or,

SITE OF DEER-PARK, excavated 1905
(Jagat Singh's stupa in the foreground.)

as his followers put it, "to turn the wheel of the Law", the Kâsis, the first Aryan settlers in the district of Benares, had become subject to the Kosâlas, who had their capital at Sâvatthi, in what is now Nepal. The Sakya, the clan to which Buddha himself belonged, were also subject to the kingdom of Kosâla. Benares had already become celebrated as a great centre of Hindu piety and learning. The old Buddhist records tell us that it had a large public hall, or pavilion, in which religious and philosophical questions were discussed. Sherring, in his *Sacred City of the Hindus* (p. 291), maintains, on very insufficient grounds, that Benares was not then, as it is now, situated between the rivers Barna and Asi, but was placed to the north of the Barna. It is more reasonable to suppose that the traces of old buildings which extend from the north of Benares towards Sarnath are the remains of the old Buddhist city which sprung up round the spot made sacred by its associations with the first preaching of Buddha, and that the Hindu city, on a much more spacious plan than it has now (for the early Aryans, as we know from Megasthenes, loved air and space in their cities), always occupied very nearly its present site.

Buddha soon found many converts, especially among the Kshatriya class, to which he belonged, and among the Bhiksus and other devotees who had not accepted the Brahminical teaching. A few members of the Sangha, or religious order which he founded, built the simple huts of recluses in the groves of the Deer-park and settled there. Many years after his death, when Asoka made Buddhism the state religion, the places hallowed by the Master's memory were marked with stone columns, and great monasteries and temples of brick and stone were built for the members of the Sangha.

The whole neighbourhood of the Deer-park became covered with votive stupas, or memorial mounds, large and small, some containing relics, others merely marking a place associated with events in the life of the Buddha, or with his numerous fabled pre-existences.

when in the form of a bird, or deer, or elephant, or human being, he was preparing, as a "Bodhisatva", by many acts of mercy and self-sacrifice, for the attainment of the final Nirvana. The smaller ones were simply devotional shrines erected by his followers as an act of piety.

MINIATURE VOTIVE SHRINE

Excavated at Sarnath, 1905, showing the sikra crowned by the amâlika ornament.

The first definite historical account of Benares and its neighbourhood is given by the Chinese pilgrim, Fa Hian, who visited India about the beginning of the 5th century A.D. for the purpose of getting exact information about the teaching of Buddha. Hiuen Thsang, another Chinese pilgrim, came about 250 years later, and has left a very interesting description of the principal stupas and monasteries as he saw them. At the north of Benares, and to the west of the Ganges, there was, he says, a stupa, or memorial tower, about 100 feet high, built by the Emperor Asoka. Near it was a stone column, highly polished and of blue colour (probably lapis lazuli), in which the reflection of Buddha might always be seen. At a distance of nearly two miles farther on, north-east from the river, he arrived at the Deer-park, where there was a monastery, built in eight sections, within a walled enclosure. There were pavilions of one and two stories for the accommodation of the monks, 1500 in number, who were studying the doctrine of the "Little Vehicle". In the midst of the enclosure was a temple-monastery, the lower part of stone, surmounted by a tower of brick faced with stone, or perhaps by the curvilinear *sikra*, or spire, similar to that of modern Jain and Hindu temples in northern India, which was crowned by the melon-shaped *amâlika* wrought in embossed gold. The amâlika formed the base of the finial.

Round about the tower, or spire, in tiers rising one over the other, were a hundred niches, each containing an image of Buddha, which Hiuen Thsang supposed to be of gold, but which were probably only of bronze or copper gilt, like those now found in Buddhist shrines and monasteries in Nepal, Sikkim, and Tibet. The temple contained a life-size statue of Buddha, made of brass, in the attitude of preaching. The illustration here given of a Nepalese Buddhist temple probably closely resembles the temple seen by Hiuen Thsang.

To the south-west of this temple was a stone stupa, built by Asoka, which had become partly buried, though it was still 100 feet in height. It was built to mark the very spot where Buddha, "having attained to perfect knowledge", began to expound to his fellow-seekers after truth the wisdom he had gained under the Bodhi tree at Gaya.

In front of it Asoka had placed a memorial column, about 70 feet high, polished like a mirror, "so that all those who pray fervently before it see from time to time, according to their petitions, figures with good or bad signs". Another stupa close by marked the place where the five disciples sat in meditation in the Isapattana Deer-park, when they reached it after their desertion of Buddha in the Vindhyan mountains. Hiuen Thsang adds that there was a multitude of sacred monuments within the enclosure of the Deer-park monastery, and describes many tanks and stupas round about it.

MODEL OF A NEPALESE BUDDHIST TEMPLE

The systematic explorations, commenced last year at Sarnath by the Archæological Department, have given a wonderful actuality to Hiuen Thsang's description. In 1794 some workmen, employed by Jagat Singh, Diwan of the Rajah of Benares, to quarry bricks from the ruins at Sarnath, hit upon a large stupa with a relic chamber, the contents of which they rifled. Archæologists of the last century supposed this to be the stupa which Asoka built in the Deer-park, and in their eagerness to find positive proof they dug out the stupa until only a mere shell was left, without result. The more scientific excavation which is now being made has already laid bare the remains of the Asoka column mentioned by Hiuen Thsang.

The principal part of the inscription is, unfortunately, missing; but the splendid lion capital in the style of ancient Persepolis is almost intact, and just as Hiuen Thsang described it, "smooth as jade and shining like a mirror". The capital probably supported the Buddhist symbols representing Buddha, the Dharma (Law), and the Sangha (congregation). At least the fragments of the wheel representing the Dharma have been discovered, and the design of the capital makes it probable that all three symbols, which correspond to the mystic syllable *aum* of the Hindu trinity, were placed above it.

The wheel is generally taken to be a special Buddhistic symbol, though it was commonly used by pre-Buddhistic philosophers to typify Life, the Universe, and also Brahman, the Universal Soul. The Upanishads say: "As the spokes of a wheel are attached to the nave, so are all things attached to Life. This Life ought to be approached with faith and reverence, and viewed as an immensity which abides in its own glory. That immensity extended from above, from below, from behind and before, from the south and from the north. It is the Soul of the Universe. It is God Himself."[1]

[1] Monier Williams: *Indian Wisdom*, p. 40.

THE ASOKA COLUMN

Marking the place where Buddha began to preach. Discovered at Sarnath, 1905

By the Buddhists the wheel came to be regarded as a symbol of their teacher's mission, and of his universal sovereignty. Under the four lions, which probably signify the four quarters, is a band panelled into four by wheels. The panels are filled with very spirited sculptures in relief of a lion, horse, bull, and elephant.

The base of the column goes deep down into the ground, and above the ancient floor-level are successive strata, on which for seventeen hundred years the devout followers of Buddha piled memorials one over the other, about the hallowed spot, until the fierce Muhammadan invaders came, bringing havoc, fire, and sword to the place where he preached gentleness, love, and peace.

The archæologists, who in the last two centuries made somewhat desultory attempts to explore the Deer-park, found everywhere traces of the great catastrophe which destroyed in one holocaust the monks, monasteries, and temples of Sarnath. Charred bones and wood, lumps of melted brass, half-fused bricks, and calcined stone testified to the fury of the invaders.

In the neighbourhood of the column there are now being unearthed the remains of important buildings, numerous votive stupas, and many beautiful Buddhist sculptures representing events in the life of the Master, or various stages in his spiritual development—portraying him as a wandering Bhiksu, sitting in meditation and in divine ecstasy, or preaching the wisdom of his enlightenment. The splendid sculpture in Chunar stone, illustrated on page 51, represents him as the preacher, expounding the truth to his fellow-Bhiksus in the Deer-park.

Among the discoveries are numbers of miniature stone shrines of non-Buddhist origin, like that figured on p. 43. Until the followers of Buddha marked the Deer-park as specially devoted to members of their order, it was a common retreat for all religious devotees, perhaps one of the ancient sacred groves left in a clearing of the virgin forest. Hiuen Thsang graphically describes what he saw in one of these forest retreats. There were Buddhists from various provinces lying in the thickets, dwelling in caves, or in huts made of leaves and branches, or under the shade of the trees. Jainas in white robes, the wandering Bhiksus, followers of Krishna, Brahmin students, ascetics undergoing various forms of self-torture, philosophers and adepts in sacrifices, and many others—all disputing, discussing, and explaining, with the tolerance of each other's views, which, at least in early times, was characteristic of Indian religious sects.

Among the Buddhist "gatakas", or birth-stories, is a pretty one, told by Hiuen Thsang, to account for this retreat of Isapattana having been specially dedicated for the protection of deer. In one of their pre-existences, Buddha and Devadatta, his cousin, were both kings of the deer, roaming a large forest near Benares. Each of them had under him a herd of a hundred head. The Raja of Benares hunted in the country round, and was destroying Devadatta's herd, so the Bodhisatva (Buddha) in pity begged of the raja that his herd might also take its turn in supplying meat for the royal kitchen. The existence of both herds would thus be prolonged.

The raja agreed, and thereafter every day a deer was drawn by lot from each herd alternately, and

BUDDHA PREACHING
Discovered at Sarnath, 1904

went voluntarily to place its head on the butcher's block. Now there was a hind in Devadatta's herd great with young, which was drawn as the next victim. She begged of the king of the herd that, for the sake of her little one, she might be passed over, but Devadatta angrily drove her away.

CARVING ON THE DHAMEK STUPA

In despair she appealed for protection to the Bodhisatva, the king of the other herd, who, filled with pity, went to the raja's palace to offer himself in her place. The people and the high officers of the court crowded to see the great king of the deer thus unexpectedly approaching. The raja's astonishment was great, and he refused to believe the news until the warder of the palace came to announce his presence at the gate. When the raja enquired of the king of the deer the reason for his sudden appearance, the latter answered: "There is a hind whose turn has come to die, but she carries a little one yet unborn. I cannot permit this wrong. I am come to offer myself in her place."

The raja, deeply touched, replied: "I am a deer in human form, you are a man in the shape of a deer". Thereupon he ordered that the slaughter of the deer should immediately cease, and that the forest where they lived should always be reserved for their protection. The name of Sarnath is said to be derived from Saranga-nath, "Lord of the Deer", one of the names of Buddha.

Until the recent remarkable discoveries were made, the chief interest of Sarnath was centred in the great ruined stupa, 110 feet high, known by the name of Dhamek, which General Cunningham derives from the Sanskrit, *Dharma-desaka*, or "preacher of the law". It was the last of the memorials built by the Buddhists within the enclosure of the Deer-park, for the rich carving of the stone-base was interrupted, probably by the first Muhammadan invasion at the beginning of the eleventh century, and never completed.

About a mile to the south of the great stupa of Dhamek is a mass of ruined brickwork, over seventy feet high, surrounded by an octagonal tower built by Humayun, the Mogul emperor, in the first half of the sixteenth century. The excavations now being made below the tower are uncovering the remains of the Buddhist stupa upon which it is built. It is believed to be the one described by Hiuen Thsang in this neighbourhood as 300 feet in height, and sparkling with the rarest and most precious materials.

Amidst all these ruined memorials of the Deer-park,

and of the great city which once flourished round about Sarnath, it is curious to note that there is only one modern temple. Strangely enough, this is not Buddhist. The missionaries of Asoka spread the Buddhist faith far and wide beyond his dominions, into the countries of Eastern Asia, where it still counts many millions of followers, but in India itself it hardly exists now

EXCAVATIONS BELOW HUMAYUN'S TOWER, SARNATH, 1905

as a separate creed. This solitary temple, close to the great stupa of Dhamek, belongs to the Jains, a sect founded by a teacher contemporary with Buddha, which still flourishes in northern India, and has many noble shrines, ancient and modern.

It is only within recent years that the history of this sect has been made clear to Europeans through the researches of Professors Jacobi, Bühler, Dr. Hoernle, and others. The founder, Mahâvîra, "the Great Hero", was a contemporary of Buddha. Like him, he was a Kshatriya of noble birth. His father, Siddartha, was the head of his clan in a petty state, the capital of which was Vaisâlî, about twenty-seven miles north of the modern Patna. Mahâvîra was born about 599 B.C., his mother being the daughter of Cetâkâ, the king.

On the death of his father, which happened when Mahâvîra was thirty years old, he, like his great contemporary, left his home and family and adopted a purely religious life, first entering the order of Paresnâth, the orthodox monastic order of his clan, and afterwards, like so many other religious devotees at that time, becoming a wandering Bhiksu, preaching new doctrines and establishing a new religious order. He imposed upon his followers the rule of absolute nudity, a rule which afterwards led to the two great divisions of the Jain sect being named the Svêtâmbaras, "the white clothed", and the Digambaras, "the unclothed". The name of the Jains is derived from the title of Jîna, or "spiritual conqueror", which was given to Mahâvîra by his followers.

The Jains hold the same tenets as the Buddhists regarding the sacredness of all life, but differ from them in accepting the orthodox Hindu view of self-mortification by bodily penances. They believe in the separate existence of the soul, which the Buddhists deny, and worship twenty-four saints, or Tirthankars, who have finished the cycles of human existences. Mahâvîra, their teacher, is considered the twenty-fourth.

Jainism is the only one of the early Indian monastic orders which has handed down almost intact its tenets and organization to the present day. The constitution of the order recognized as members, not only the monks and nuns who took the vows, but it also admitted as lay brothers and sisters all who supported the religious institutions of the Jain community. When the Buddhist religious houses declined in influence, the looseness of the ties which attached their lay adherents to them caused the latter to revert easily to their traditional spiritual leaders. The whole organization thus gradually broke to pieces. The Jains, on the other hand, being a much more homogeneous body, survived the period of the Brahmin supremacy and the persecution of Muhammadan rule. They have maintained their institutions intact for over two thousand years, while Buddhism, as a distinct sect, gradually disappeared from India and became merged in the various Vaishnavite sects which grew into prominence about the twelfth and thirteenth centuries.

CHAPTER IV

THE RISE OF MODERN HINDUISM

As Benares never played an important part in the strife between the ancient kingdoms of northern India, it is extremely difficult to ascertain any precise details of its history from the time of the preaching of Buddha down to the rise of modern Hinduism. We only know that the Kosâla kingdom, which had absorbed the Kâsî clan, the first Aryan settlers at Benares, was, about B.C. 300, itself absorbed by the great empire of Magadha, which had its capital at Pâtaliputra, the modern Patna. Asoka, the third emperor of the Magadha dynasty, became a member of the Buddhist order, or *Sangha*, made Buddhism the state religion, and sent missionaries to Kashmir, the Himalayan regions, Afghanistan, Burma, southern India, and Ceylon. He built magnificent stupas and monasteries at Sarnath and many other places. It is probable that Benares itself greatly diminished in importance during the Buddhist supremacy, as the followers of Buddha naturally esteemed most sacred the Deer-park and the places in the neighbourhood of Sarnath, hallowed by the associations of their great teacher.

The legends of Divodâs, as recorded in the Kâsî-khanda, the mythical history of Benares by an unknown Brahmin writer, probably refer to the occupation of the city by Buddhist rulers. It is said that Divodâs, having been made Raja of Benares by Brahmâ, expelled Shiva and all the other Hindu gods from the city. He was a man of spotless purity; and, being an adept in the science of sacrifice, the efforts of the gods to evict him were for a long time unavailing. Brahmâ, disguised as a Brahmin ascetic, managed to obtain permission to reside there; but it was not until Ganêsha, the god of wisdom, got the better of Divodâs by a clever trick, that Shiva and the other gods were at last reinstated.

Asoka himself was no bigot or persecutor. In one of his famous Rock Edicts, or proclamations of the Faith, he enjoins that no one should seek to disparage other sects in order to exalt his own. "Let a man seek rather after the growth in his own sect of the essence of the matter"[1]—noble sentiments which might well be considered by the followers of all creeds. It is probable, therefore, that such of the Brahmins and other Hindus who refused to accept the teaching of Buddha were left in undisturbed possession of their holy places at Benares.

Buddha's philosophy and simple rule of life were not exempt from the modifications which all religious doctrines undergo at the hands of their successive interpreters. Popular superstition soon invested Buddha's person with miraculous powers, to which he himself laid no claim, and after his death the thaumaturgic powers of the Brahmin priesthood, which he contemptuously disputed, were associated with his own relics. Kings went to war over the possession of his water-pot, his sweeping-brush, his tooth, hairs, or

[1] Rock Edict, No. 12. See Rhys David's *Buddhist India*, p. 296.

pieces of his nails. The sanctity attached to his own person and acts were extended by extravagant tales of his former existences, when, as a Bodhisatva, or potential Buddha, he was preparing himself for the final enlightenment, in the form of a bird, a deer, or six-tusked elephant.

Hiuen Thsang in the seventh century describes a stupa containing an eyeball of Buddha "as large as an âmra fruit, and so bright that its rays dart forth from the base to some distance outside",[1] and repeats as worthy of credit stories of wild elephants bringing offerings to his relic shrines. Similar legends may be seen sculptured on the Buddhist monuments at Bharhut and Sanchi, which were erected within three centuries after the death of Buddha. The practice of divination and sorcery, which formed no part of Buddha's creed, became as popular with his disciples as they had been with the Brahmin priests. In short, the very errors which Buddha had tried to eradicate became a part of his followers' beliefs and the starting-point of new religious reformers.

Owing to the great diversity of racial types in India, thrown together, yet differing in an extraordinary degree in intellectual and social development, there have always been two main currents, of religious evolution and devolution—more clearly distinguishable than in other countries—moving in opposite directions, yet insensibly affecting each other. The high ideals of Buddha's Eight-fold Path were gradually lost in the current of popular superstitions, but nevertheless they purified the muddy waters of priestcraft and cleared away many obstructions to the progress of true re-

[1] *Life of Hiuen Thsang.* S. Beal, p. 59.

ligion. Buddha became absorbed in the Hindu pantheon as one of the incarnations of Vishnu, the Preserver, but when about the eighth century Brahminism succeeded in reasserting its authority, the whole of its spiritual teaching was permeated with the doctrines of a purer and nobler faith.

Benares again became the centre of religious activity in northern India with the appearance of the great Hindu reformer, Sankaracharya. It would be travelling beyond my province to enter into a discussion of the details of his life and doctrines. It will be sufficient to briefly indicate the changes which had come over Brahminical religious practices and ideas in the thirteen centuries which had elapsed since the death of Buddha. The slaughter of animals as a part of sacrificial rites had almost ceased, or was practised only by some of the lowest castes. Sacrifice had lost a great deal of its pretended magical virtue, and acquired more of symbolical significance as applied to spiritual advancement by the suppression of carnal appetite and worldly desires. In the hymn now chanted by the Smarta Brahmins, the modern disciples of Sankaracharya, before breaking fast, occur the following lines on "the sacrifice of self":—

"And of the sacrifice performed by the master who has understood these truths, the soul is the performer; the heart, the seat of the sacrificial fire; sensual desires, the ghee; anger, the sacrificial lamb; contemplation, fire; the period of sacrifice, as long as life shall last; whatsoever is drunk, the soma drink; and death, the sacred bath which finishes the ceremony".[1]

The vague speculations of the early Aryans regard-

[1] *Sri Sankaracharya, his Life and Times.* By Krishnaswami Aiyar.

ing the nature of the soul and the origin of the universe had resolved themselves into definite shape as the six schools or *darsanas* of philosophy, all taking for their foundation the axiom that *ex nihilo nihil fit*, and all directed to one end—the cessation of the cycle of re-births and absorption of the soul of man into the one Supreme Soul. They also agree in recognizing the operation of the law of *karma*, adopted by Buddha, through which every human action is held to entail a consequence upon the agent, good or evil according to the character of the action, which follows him or her through the whole cycle of transmigrations.

The caste system had become firmly established, and the Brahmins had assumed extravagant pretensions to spiritual superiority, but the creed of the lower classes had been raised to a distinctly higher plane by the doctrines of the Bhagavat Gita, "The Song of the Blessed One"; incorporated with the Mahâbhârata, probably in the first few centuries of the Christian era. The idea of a personal God, as creator and preserver of the universe, its high moral standard and the similarity of some of its passages to the New Testament, have caused many Christian missionaries to attribute the Bhagavat Gita to the influence of early Christian converts, and to intellectual intercourse between India and the schools of Alexandria. Max Müller and other Sanskrit authorities reject this theory. However this may be, the Bhagavat Gita is now by far the most popular of all Brahminical sacred writings. It is translated into all the principal vernaculars. Pocket editions of it are carried about by Hindus of all classes, just as devout Christians may carry the Bible. It has undoubtedly profoundly influenced the ethical and spiritual ideas of modern Hinduism.

Sankaracharya waged relentless war against the superstitions of the Buddhists of his time, and against the loathsome practices of some of the Hindu sects; but convinced of the futility of attempting to supersede entirely the ancient forms of popular worship by the high philosophic doctrines of the intellectual Brahmins, he effected a compromise. Buddha had established an ethical code which afforded a common meeting-ground for all races, classes, and sects of Hindus, but had left untouched the problems of the first Cause and the directing Power of the Universe. Sankaracharya and other Brahmin teachers provided a common metaphysical basis for all popular religious beliefs, while allowing the widest latitude for various forms of worship.

It is not to be supposed that Sankaracharya was the first to teach the pantheistic doctrines of Hinduism. The idea of the One Supreme Being manifested in the many had been clearly indicated centuries before in the Upanishads, and developed in the Vedanta school of philosophy, but Sankaracharya's preaching marks the final absorption of Buddhism into the Brahminical system, and the development of the worship of Shiva into one of the most popular cults. Shiva-worship had indeed existed long before the eighth century, and perhaps is older than Hinduism itself. One of Shiva's names, Rudra, is the name of the Vedic storm-god. Shiva is mentioned several times in the Mahâbhârata, and we learn from Hiuen Thsang that in the first half of the seventh century Shiva was already the principal deity of Benares. Nevertheless it was

Sankaracharya's teaching and philosophy which established Shivaism, for the time being, as the principal sect of Hinduism.

The Buddhist monasteries continued to exist at Sarnath, and elsewhere in India, until they were finally destroyed by the Muhammadan invaders of the thirteenth century; but in the eighth century Buddhism as a separate religion was already discredited, and the Brahmins were reinstated in their position as the spiritual leaders of the people. After the establishment of Muhammadan rule the popularity of the cult of Shiva, as expounded by Sankaracharya, diminished, and many new sects successively developed in which the worship of Vishnu and the idea of a personal God became more prominent. It is, however, impossible to follow the further development of Hinduism through all the different phases which have originated, and are still creating, new sects and schools of thought. We must now pass on to a brief study of the ideas of modern Hinduism as conveyed in the worship of Shiva, the presiding deity of Benares.

It will be understood from the preceding sketch that, through the absorption of many primitive faiths and modes of worship into the Brahminical system, there is often a very wide difference between the popular views regarding the various Hindu divinities and the esoteric teaching of the Brahmin philosophy. The stories told in the Puranas and other later Sanskrit literature embody the wildest legends and superstitions, and attribute to Hindu gods and goddesses an abundant share of earthly passions and weaknesses. Many of these seeming fantastic stories are, however, metaphysical ideas conveyed in the form of allegory.

According to the esoteric doctrine of Hinduism, first propounded in the Rig-Veda, the universe was originally Soul only, nothing else whatsoever existed, active or inactive. The origin of Creation, described in the famous hymn of the Rig-Veda (X, 129), proceeded from this Supreme Spirit, the Eternal Essence, or Brahman.

The first manifestation of this neuter Brahman—the Unknowable—when passing into a conditioned state, comparable to the passing of a human being from a state of profound sleep to a state of dreaming and then of waking, is known as Ishwara—the Self—the Lord and Cause of all things. The glory of Ishwara as *Purusha*, or Spirit, makes manifest *Prakriti*, the Essence of Matter, inherent in Brahman, but until now unmanifested. Ishwara, then, by means of his divine power, called *sakti*, causes Prakriti to take form. The forms of Prakriti thus evolved are the Trimurti, or Three Aspects of Ishwara—Brahmâ, who in the world of Matter performs the functions of Creator, and represents the condition of activity or motion; Vishnu, who is the Preserver, representing equilibrium and rhythm; and Shiva, who is the dissolving power. In Hindu painting and sculpture this act in the great drama of creation is represented by Ishwara, under the name of Nârâyana, floating on the waters of chaos and sleeping on the serpent Sesha, or Ananta, "the endless"—the symbol of eternity—while Brahmâ, the Creator, springs from a lotus flower which is growing from Ishwara's navel.

The Trimurti, as representing Spirit-essence, have different qualities or conditions (gunas). Brahmâ represents the quality of Being; Vishnu, Thought-power; and Shiva, the quality of Bliss, the perfect beatitude of Nirvana. Purusha and Prakriti being inert by themselves, each of the Trimurti have their *saktis*, or divine powers, which enable them to perform their functions in the universe. In popular Hinduism the *saktis* are regarded as the wives of the Trimurti. The *sakti* of Brahmâ is deified as Saraswati, the goddess of learning and wisdom; the *sakti* of Vishnu is Lakshmi, the goddess of prosperity; and the *sakti* of Shiva, Durgâ, Gaurî, or Kâlî, terrible goddesses to whom bloody sacrifices, and sometimes human victims, are offered.

The worship of Brahmâ has almost ceased as a popular religion, because his work in the universe is considered to be finished. Shiva is the presiding deity at Benares, and all the principal temples are dedicated to him. But Shiva at Benares is Mahâdeva, the great god, or Ishwara, representing the powers of all the Trimurti; for the followers of particular cults, like that of Shiva, Vishnu, or of Kâlî, generally ascribe to their special deity the exercise of all the divine functions. It must also be noted that each one of the Trimurti, besides the two main qualities, or *gunas*, attributed to him, has countless sub-manifestations corresponding to the infinite subdivisions of their duties in the cosmic order. Thus there are hundreds of temples and shrines at Benares with names ending in "-eshwar" (Ishwara), such as Tarak-eshwar, Ratn-eshwar, Som-eshwar, &c., all of which are Shiva temples dedicated to some particular manifestation of the Supreme Ishwara. The Hindu pantheon is estimated to contain 300,000,000 deities, but the Brahminical teaching clearly explains them as indicating the infinite manifestations of the One Supreme.

It is a difficult matter for a European observer to ascertain how far the philosophical doctrines of Hinduism are comprehended by the mass of the people. On this point I do not venture to express an opinion, but only quote two very competent witnesses. Dr. Lefroy, Bishop of Lahore, in a recent sermon said: "From a long personal experience I can bear witness to the extraordinary aptitude with which they engage in discussion or speculation on the deepest philosophical and ethical questions—and that not merely in the case of the upper, or more educated classes, but not infrequently in the case of the very poorest and wholly illiterate persons as well".

Mr. Burns, who made special enquiries during the last census regarding the beliefs of the common people, says: "The general result of my enquiries is that the great majority of Hindus have a firm belief in one Supreme God, called Bhagwan, Parameshwar, Ishwar, or Narain. Mr. Baillie made some enquiries, which showed that this involved a clear idea of a single personal God. I am inclined to think that this is not limited to the more intelligent, but is distinctly characteristic of Hindus as a whole." (*Census Report*, 1901, vol. i. part 1, p. 303.)

Shiva, in popular Hinduism, is the great white-faced Ascetic of the Himalayas, representing the life of austerity which the Brahmins point out as one of the roads to Shiva's abodes of bliss and ultimate absorption into the Absolute. He has three eyes, which are explained variously as the Trimurti, the three Vedas, and the power of seeing the past, present, and future. Two of the epithets applied to him, "the moon-crested" and "blue-throated", will be very suggestive to those who have watched the crescent moon rising over the great Himalayan snow-peaks, and seen the wonderful tints of violet-blue just below the snow-line at sunrise. The five heads which he generally has are the five sacred rivers which flow from the Himalayas. In his temples at Benares he is only represented by the phallic emblems, the symbol of his reproductive power by which, as Ishwara, he created Brahmâ, Vishnu, and himself. The same symbol was used by the Egyptians in the worship of Osiris, and by the ancient Greeks to signify the first principle of animation.

It has been suspected that the lingam was borrowed by the Brahmins from the ritual of some non-Aryan cult, but if so, lingam-worship must have been incorporated with the Aryan religion at a very early period, as both the Aitareya and Taittirîya Upanishads contain references to it,[1] enjoining phallic worship as a step leading to a knowledge of the Absolute. But it is a mistake to suppose that Shiva worship, as a whole, countenances sensuality. On the contrary, Shiva is always regarded as an example and type of austerity; the grosser forms of Hindu worship are chiefly found in the Sâkta sects, and in the cults of Vishnu.

In the Madras Presidency Shiva is most frequently worshipped in his aspect as Natesa, "the Dancer", the Lord of Bliss, and manifestation of Purusha, "Spirit". A splendid bronze, now in the Madras Museum, shows that Hindu sculptors have not always been so deficient in the higher qualities of artistic expression as is generally supposed. Shiva, sur-

[1] Ait., p. 83, and Taitt., p 110. (Anandâsram Edit.)

rounded by a halo or glory of fire (representing the energy of heat by which Ishwara was evolved from the Supreme Brahman), is dancing on a prostrate

SHIVA, AS NATESA

From a bronze in the Madras Museum.

Asura, a spirit of evil. In one hand he holds a drum to scare away evil spirits, and in another the sacrificial fire which leads to heaven. He wears a tiara, behind which a number of cobras issue, forming fantastic streamers on either side of his head.

In the Brahmanas the serpent is said to signify that the evil of the body can be put off by means of sacrifice, just as a serpent throws off its dead skin. It also symbolizes the doctrine of transmigration, the idea of the human soul obtaining release through a series of changes of the body. Perhaps, also, it symbolizes the reproductive power of Shiva, as the snake is popularly supposed to renew its body every time it casts its skin.

The movement and modelling of this ancient bronze are superb. There is something of classic feeling in the boldness of the generalization shown in the technique, and even the monstrous addition of four arms is treated with so much artistic skill as to make it inoffensive. There is no figure sculpture of this quality to be found in Benares except in the old Buddhist art, where the same feeling is sometimes shown. The iconoclastic zeal of Aurangzîb, who enforced the strict Muhammadan law against the representation of animate nature in art, is still felt in all the art of northern India.

CHAPTER V

IN THE CITY

The sacred character which Hindus ascribe to Benares is not confined to the precincts of the city. The influence of the patron deity extends to the whole area, shaped roughly like the crescent moon placed over Shiva's head, which is contained by the bank of the Ganges between its little tributaries, Barna on the north and Asi on the south, and by the Panch-kôsi road. The latter describes a rough semicircle round the city, the centre being the Manikarnika well, the first place of pilgrimage, and the radius a distance of five kôs, or about ten miles.

The sacrificial virtue of Shiva's city is no doubt enhanced by the circumstance that the Ganges at this point takes a great sweep round, so that its current while it passes Benares is flowing in a northerly direction, or towards the Himalayas, where Shiva is said to dwell. The aspect of the river-front of the city facing the rising sun was another point which may have guided the choice of the early Aryan or pre-Aryan sun-worshippers. In ancient Hindu sculptures, Surya, the sun-god, is generally associated with the gods of the later Trimurti — Brahmâ, Vishnu, and Shiva.

In the good old days the city was reached either

by the river or by the Grand Trunk road, and even now devout pilgrims approach it by the ways which millions of pious Hindus have followed for centuries on centuries, either by cart or boat, or on foot. A few devotees, in fulfilment of a vow, will painfully prostrate themselves at full length, and day after day, and month after month, mark the weary way with their bodies, believing that the penance will obtain for them a great store of merit, both in this existence and in the hereafter. At the first sight of the holy city they will salute it with shouts of "Jai! Jai! Kâsinath!" ("Hail! Hail! Lord of Kâsi!"), the latter being the name of the southern quarter, which is popularly applied to the whole city of Benares.

Europeans, and the great majority of Hindus, now come to Benares by the railway. It is amusing to see sometimes at Mogul Serai, the junction for the East Indian line, how the up-to-date Indian arriving from Calcutta, Bombay, or some other large Anglo-Indian city, will in an incredibly short time divest himself of his European environment and transform himself into the orthodox Hindu. You will see him first stepping out of the train, dressed in more or less correct European garb, and smoking a cigarette. He is accompanied by a servant, who deposits a steel trunk on the platform in front of him. Then, *coram populo*, but without the least suggestion of impropriety, he proceeds to take off coat, waistcoat, trousers, and boots, and taking out of the trunk a collection of spotless white drapery, speedily arrays himself in *puggaree*, *dhotee*, and the rest of the becoming costume of an Indian gentleman, while the cast-off garments are stowed away until his next return to European society.

He is now a good Hindu, fit to appear in the holy city.

Benares cantonment is, like many other Anglo-Indian stations, a collection of bungalows, with the usual barracks, club, court-houses, offices, official residences, and hotels. It is not until one reaches the Chowk, the principal thoroughfare in the city proper, and its continuations on the north and south, that it is possible to realize the part which Benares plays in the religious life of India. The whole of the ground between this main road and the river is a labyrinth of lanes and alleys, only wide enough for foot traffic, which contains innumerable temples, shrines, and holy places, full of associations for the Hindu worshipper.

In the early morning, especially when it is a Hindu festival, or on a day esteemed propitious for the sacred bath, Sannyâsin in their ochre robes, nearly naked fakirs, pilgrims from every corner of India, men, women, and children, hurry to and fro, jostling with goats and the sacred bulls and cows—fat and sleek and too well fed to thoroughly appreciate the freedom of the city, which is accorded to them as representatives of the gods. At every few yards there is a temple, or a shrine, on which passers-by will sprinkle holy Ganges water or place a garland. The brass-shops are filled with vessels for use in the daily religious ceremonies and idols worshipped in Hindu households. There are flower-shops which sell the floral offerings to the deities—wreaths of golden marigold or white jessamine, pink rose-petals, and crimson hibiscus flowers, and the leaves of the bêl-tree, shaped like Shiva's trident. Others deal in all sorts of mysterious Hindu symbols and objects of worship; rosaries used by the followers of Shiva and Vishnu, and the sacred thread worn by the twice-born castes.

The holy fish which saved Manu from the flood, a symbol of good luck, and the lion vehicle of the goddess Durgâ, are carved on every house and shop-

THE GODDESS DURGÂ—A FRESCO PAINTING

front; quaint paintings of the gods and goddesses, of Râma and Sîtâ, and the great combats of the Mahâbhârata, decorate the walls. In every corner where a tree will grow the sacred pippal and banian find a place, and under their spreading branches a heap of carved stones, fragments from ancient temples, are set up for worship.

It is not difficult to find the way through this network of narrow lanes, once it is realized that they all trend in one of two directions, towards the river or parallel to it. On the river-front they nearly all end in gigantic flights of stone steps leading down to the bathing-ghâts, for the city is built on a high ridge about a hundred feet above the river. After the monsoon floods have subsided, the base of these great pyramids of steps gets wider and wider, as the water shrinks, until in the hot season the foundations of the ghâts, or what Pierre Loti has picturesquely called "the roots of the city", are laid bare. In the rains the Ganges rushes past Benares in a mighty stream, covering the whole of the ghâts and filling the countless small shrines, which are built in and upon them, with a thick deposit of silt. The basement of the great palaces which line the river-bank are then flooded, and the daily bath in the sacred river is taken within the building, convenient recesses for the bathers being arranged along the main staircase.

Compared with many other Indian cities, there is not much of architectural interest in Benares except these palaces, which have been built by Hindu princes and nobles, but are rarely occupied by them, and chiefly serve as asylums for their old retainers, who are given the privilege of spending their last days in Shiva's city, so that when they die they may be transported at once to Shiva-loka, the abode of bliss. There is a great deal of picturesqueness in the narrow alleys, but, if it were not for the temples and the people, it would be easy to imagine one's self to be wandering in an old town of Spain or southern Italy. Neither do the temples by any means represent, either in constructive design or in ornament, the best that Indian architects have produced. Nearly all are of quite modern date, very few of the more important ones being older than the eighteenth century.

The Afghans, who in 1194 A.D. burnt the Buddhist monasteries at Sarnath, probably laid waste Benares also. Alâuddîn, about 1300 A.D., is said to have destroyed a thousand temples. During the tolerant rule of Akbar and of the earlier Mogul emperors, the city may have recovered some of the splendour which it had in the palmy days of Hindu rule, but Aurangzîb in the seventeenth century levelled the temples to the ground and caused several mosques to be built with the materials. The great mosque above Panchganga ghât, whose lofty minarets dominate the whole city, is one of the memorials of his intolerant zeal.

The northern part of Benares contains a few remains of ancient temples, mostly converted into Muhammadan mosques, but in the heart of the city the only vestiges of its former architectural magnificence, besides the ruins of the old Vishweshwar temple which are behind another of Aurangzîb's mosques near the Golden Temple, are fragments of carvings built into walls, or set up for worship under a sacred tree and within the temples. The sculptured records of ancient times afford plenty of scope for the student and archæologist who may try to piece together the fragmentary history of Benares, but to the Hindu worshipper they only symbolize the foundation of his creed—the One in Many. There is always room in his pantheon for divinities, new or old, strange or familiar. In Benares there are fifteen hundred Hindu temples, and the smaller shrines are countless; but though bearing hundreds of different names, they are all, with the exception of a few dedicated to Vishnu, recognized as

A BENARES STREET

belonging to Mahâdeva, "the great god", meaning Ishwara, or Shiva, and are surmounted by his trident, the symbol of the Hindu trinity. Even Vishnu is regarded by his devotees only as another name for Ishwara.

The doctrine of the One in Many is symbolized by the peculiar construction of the temple spires. They

A VILLAGE TEMPLE IN BENGAL

are mostly of one type, the form of which was probably derived from an ancient Aryan tent or hut, or from some primitive non-Aryan fetish shrine. The curvilinear form in ancient times was no doubt formed of bamboos tied together at the top and strengthened with shorter horizontal pieces. The roof covering was of thatch, palm leaves, or skins. Afterwards the stonemasons found it easy to imitate this construction with slabs of the sandstones which abound in the Ganges valley. The type of stone temple which they first evolved is shown in the illustration of an ancient village temple in the Santhal Parganas of Bengal. This was later on elaborated into the multiform temple spire, found all over the Ganges valley, which is the usual type at Benares. By breaking up the main form into innumerable smaller spires, while still retaining

GÂI GHÂT—A CLASSIC GROUP (see page 155)

the constructive unity, the Brahmins enforced the teaching of their philosophic doctrines.

But it is not in its architectural features that the chief attraction of Benares lies. It is as a microcosm of Indian life, customs, and popular beliefs that it furnishes a never-ending fascination. Here the student may read a living commentary, more convincing than any record ever written, painted, or sculptured, of the life of ancient Egypt, Babylon, Nineveh, and Greece. Here the artist may see before him in the flesh the models of classic sculptors and painters, which might have served for the Panathenaic frieze, the statuettes of Tanagra, and the frescoes of Pompeii. There is an indescribable charm of colour in the throng of women on the ghâts and in the streets—the rainbow-tinted cotton saris of the United Provinces, with their varied shades of lemon, rose, and the palest blue, contrasting with the simple white of Bengal and the deeper notes of indigo, crimson, orange, and chestnut from the rich silks of the Deccan and southern India. The painter need not search for subjects; he will rather be bewildered by the kaleidoscope of changing scenes, groups, and incidents, with marvellous backgrounds and surroundings, which pass before him in endless succession.

You may spend hours on the ghâts and in the streets and temples watching the old-world customs and the simple faith of the common people, who, however misguided, show an earnestness and deep religious feeling which many conventional Christians might study with advantage. It must not be supposed that this faith and piety are common to all Hindus in the holy city. Unless report maligns them, there are many Brahmin priests in Benares leading immoral lives, and waxing rich and fat on the offerings of the pilgrims. It is certainly evident that many of those in charge of the temples, and more especially the low-class Brahmin *Ganga-putras*, or "sons of the Ganges", who act as guides and instructors to the ignorant pilgrim-folk, are more concerned in extracting money from the worshippers, and in pestering tourists, than in attending to their religious duties. Shares in temple property, which carry with them the disposal of the pilgrims' offerings, are often bought and sold like common merchandise. It is even said that a proprietary right in a Hindu temple has in this way sometimes fallen into Muhammadan hands.

If, moreover, an index to a people's feelings is always to be found in their art, it is worth noting that there is a vast difference in the artistic quality of the popular art of the present day and that of fifty

AN OLD SACRIFICIAL VESSEL

years ago. It is not only in the attempts of the wealthier classes to imitate vulgar European fashions that the degradation of Indian art is visible. Even in the art which springs from the religious life of the people, in their idols and sacrificial vessels, there is a marked absence of the sincerity and depth of feeling which are conspicuous in the older work.

But it would not be wise to attach too much significance to this deterioration, and to assume that less devotion to signs and symbols implies a giving way of the foundations of Hindu beliefs. Idolatry and symbolic ritual were never regarded as indispensable to Hinduism, but rather as a kind of spiritual *kindergarten* to help the masses to understand the abstract ideas of Brahmin philosophy. Hindu reformers have been as earnest as Christian missionaries in denouncing them, and it would be a fatal mistake if the latter believed that by the uprooting of idolatry India must needs become Christian.

It must, however, always be a matter for astonishment that cultured Hindus of great intellectual attain-

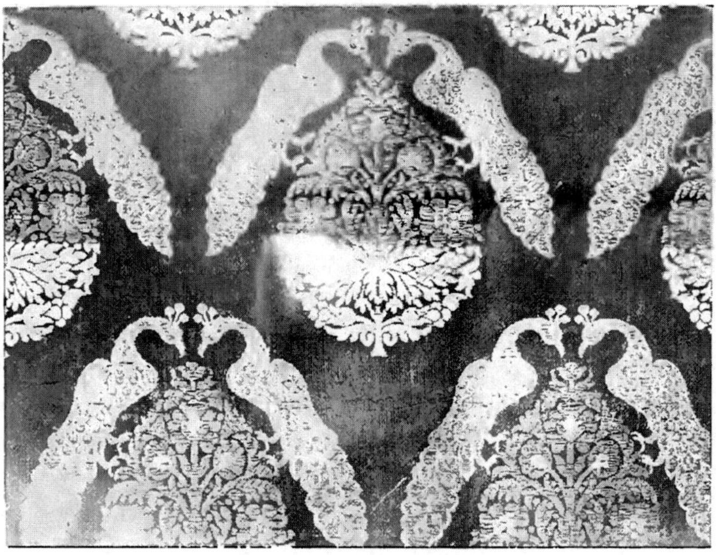

AN OLD BENARES BROCADE

ments should regard as adequate symbols of their high philosophic abstractions the vulgar dolls and childish paraphernalia which now, at Benares and elsewhere, take the place of the fine sculpture and splendid art of former days.

It is remarkable that the art industry for which Benares has long been famous, the weaving of silks and kincobs, or silk brocades, is now principally in the hands of Muhammadan weavers. Whether they were converted to Islam in the Mogul times, forcibly or from motives of self-interest, is not apparently known. Benares has probably been a seat of the industry from the earliest times, but it is more than likely that during the Muhammadan invasions the best artisans were frequently deported for the service of the victors' courts. Similarly, when Mogul rule was firmly established in India, there may have been frequent importations of artisans from the great cities of Persia and Central Asia.

Gold and silver brocade was originally made of thin strips of gold or silver woven into linen or cotton. Silk was already in use in India in the times of the Mahâbhârata and Râmâyana, and has always been more worn by Hindus than Muhammadans, for whereas the former consider it purer than cotton for ceremonial purposes, so that it can be used at meal-times without being washed, the latter prohibited the use of it as too effeminate for men's garments unless mixed with cotton. This restriction was, however, relaxed in cold weather and in time of war, on account of the better protection afforded by heavy silks and brocades. A plague of lice was also held to justify the use of silk by the strict Musalman.

The mixed fabric of silk and cotton, dyed in variegated colours, and woven in various zigzag stripes, is called *mashru*, or "lawful". It is still made at Benares for Muhammadan men's garments, but it is a decaying industry. Jains and strict Hindus who object to the wilful destruction of any forms of life wear a coarse silk made from cocoons from which the moth has escaped.

In the Mogul times there was at every court a

manufacture of magnificent silks and brocades worn by the sultans and their wives, and by the nobles and their wives. Muhammad Tuglak, in the fourteenth century, kept at Delhi 500 weavers to make the gold brocades worn by his wives, and lavishly distributed as royal presents.

Under British rule the demand for these gorgeous fabrics has greatly decreased, but compared with other textiles the *kincob* industry is fairly flourishing, though not free from the bane of aniline dyes and European patterns. Lately, however, some of the manufacturers have wisely set themselves to reproduce a number of fine old patterns found in the palace of the Maharajah of Benares.

AN OLD BENARES LOTA

The other great art craft of Benares is the metal-work, including the manufacture of brass and copper idols, lamps, and sacrificial utensils, and all sorts of native cooking and drinking vessels which fill the brass bazaar. The most characteristic are the *lotas* for Ganges water, made of brass and overlaid with copper, and chased with mythological figures and emblems of Shiva or Vishnu; the brass representing the river Jumna and the copper the Ganges. The old discarded vessels, which are sold as *purâna chîz*, are always far better than the new.

The Hindu idea of the sacrificial purity of copper water-vessels is interesting in view of a statement recently made in the *Indian Medical Journal*, that water kept in clean copper vessels for twenty-four hours is probably rendered safe for drinking purposes. Every Hindu villager prefers untinned copper vessels for bringing drinking-water from the well.

The Benares brassware, made specially for Europeans, is a pitiful example of the vulgarity and inanity to which Indian art can descend when the modern commercial element is brought into it, and when it is out of touch with the religious ideas on which its whole foundation rests. It is, unfortunately, made too familiar by Indian exhibitions and curiosity shops to need any description.

In the Hindu social and religious system the musicians and dancing-girls are an indispensable institution. They personate the Gandharvas, the mythical musicians of Indra's heaven, who attend the feasts of the gods, and the Apsarases, the voluptuous charmers—

> "With all the gifts of grace, of youth, and beauty.
> . . . . Yet thus fair,
> Nor god nor demon sought their wedded love." [1]

The dancing-girls of Benares are generally the unmarried daughters of the *Kathak* caste—the caste of professional musicians. They live in the quarter known as the Dâl-ki-mandi, a long street with houses of several stories, some of them resplendent with silver

[1] *Râmâyana.* Wilson's translation.

furniture and crystal chandeliers. Unlike the dancing-girls of southern India, they are not attached to any particular temple, or "married to the god", but at special festivals or religious ceremonies they are engaged to chant the praises of Râma, or to sing Sîtâ's love, in the classic songs of Tulsi Dâs, or the more voluptuous odes which tell of Krishna and his amours. Of secular songs for pleasure-parties they have an extensive repertoire, both old and modern. They are often very generous with the wealth they acquire, and in old age, when virtue has become a necessity, spend it freely in works of charity and religion.

Benares from very ancient times has been famed for these sirens, whose amorous glances, alluring mimic, and pretty shuffling feet have troubled many a Hindu sage. Among the many stories of Buddha's former existences is one which explains why he deserted his faithful wife, Yasodhara. It was the retribution for a crime she had committed in a former life, when she was a dancing-girl at Benares.

Long years before, the story goes,[1] there was a young and handsome horse-dealer, named Vajrasena, who lived at Takshasila. As he was going to the fair at Varanâsî (Benares), he was attacked by a gang of dacoits, who stole his horses and severely wounded him. He crawled for shelter into a deserted house in the suburbs of the city, where he was found by the watchmen and arrested as a thief. The next day he was brought before the raja, and in spite of his protestations of innocence was condemned to death. But on his way to prison he was seen by Syama, the first dancing-girl of Benares, who fell madly in love with

[1] See *Nepalese Buddhist Literature*, p. 135. By Rajendra Lala Mitra.

TEMPLE AT DASÂSAMEDH GHÂT

his manly beauty. She gave orders to her handmaids that he was to be rescued at all hazards. They offered large bribes to the executioners, who agreed to set Vajrasena free if Syama would arrange for a substitute to suffer the death penalty in his place.

Now, Syama had an admirer, a rich banker's son.

Pretending that Vajrasena was her relative, she persuaded him, out of love for her, to take some refreshment to the condemned man. He went to the execution-ground without the least suspicion of any treachery, and, as he was approaching Vajrasena, the executioners, according to the prearranged plan, suddenly cut him in two. Vajrasena was hurried off to the house of Syama by her handmaids.

Syama's passion for Vajrasena grew deeper and deeper, but he could never forget her infamous conduct towards the banker's son, and sought means to escape from her seductive snares. At last the opportunity came when they both went down to the Ganges for a pleasure excursion. Vajrasena plied her with wine, and when she was quite overcome he smothered her, and held her under the water until he believed her dead. Then he dragged the lifeless body to the steps of the ghâts, and fled away to his home in Takshasila.

Syama's mother, however, happened to be near at hand, and with great exertions restored her daughter to life. The first step Syama took after her recovery was to seek a Bhiksuin (a female devotee) of Takshasila, and to send through her a message to Vajrasena assuring him of her undying love and imploring him to return.

Buddha was that Vajrasena, and Syama, Yasodhara.

CHAPTER VI

ON THE GANGES

"*Arise! The breath of life hath come back to us—the darkness is gone, the light approacheth! Ushas hath opened a path for Surya, the Sun, to travel; now our days will be lengthened. Singing the praises of the brightening morn, the priest, the poet, ariseth with the web of his hymn. Bounteous maiden, shine upon him who praiseth thee; spread upon us the gift of life and children, thou who givest heroic sons and wealth of kine and horses. . . . Mother of the gods! Revelation of the glory of the Infinite! Banner of sacrifice, magnificent Ushas, shine forth—arise! Shower thy blessings upon our prayers, and make us chief among the people.*"—
Rig-Veda, Hymn to the Dawn, I. 113.

The traveller who wishes to realize the magnificence of Benares on the river-side, and to catch some reflection of that Vedic brightness which still shines through all that is sordid and vulgar in the modern city, must be at Dasâsamedh Ghât before the first streak of dawn. This is what he may see as he floats slowly down the river on a December morning:—

There is a coppery glow on the eastern horizon; the Ashvins, twin heralds of the dawn, are rising. Curling wreaths of evaporation rise from the placid river, and a blanket of white mist lies over the great sandy waste, laid bare by the shrinking of the monsoon flood. King Soma, the Moon, is sinking slowly behind the ghâts, and in the dim light of his silvery rays the massive monasteries and palaces, built by devout Hindu princes, loom mysteriously out of the mist, and seem to rise like a gigantic fortress wall, sheer from the water's edge. A few boats are crossing the river,

"Lighting up the recesses of the cave-like shrines"

bringing passengers to the holy city from the unhallowed ground on the opposite shore, where no Hindu will care to die, for fear of being re-incarnated as an ass.

The light brightens as Ushas, the lovely dawn-maiden, beloved of the Vedic poets, clad in robes of saffron and rose-colour, throws open the doors of the sky. Now the details of the ghâts can be more clearly distinguished—the colossal flights of stone steps, great stone piers and wooden platforms jutting out into the sacred stream, dotted over with palm-leaf umbrellas, like gigantic toad-stools, under which the *ghâliyas* are sitting to render various services to the bathers—the countless spires of Hindu temples, dominated by the lofty minarets of Aurangzib's mosque. At last, Surya, the Sun, appears, glowing with opal fire above the cloudy bars of night. The miasmatic mists, like evil spirits—the wicked Asuras—shrink and shrivel and vanish into thin air, as he pierces them through and through and flings his victorious rays across the river, lighting up the recesses of the cave-like shrines, flashing on the brass and copper vessels of the bathers and on the gilded metal flags and crescents which surmount the temples of Shiva. It seems, at first, as if the whole amphitheatre, about two miles in circuit, glittering in the sunlight, were one vast sun-temple: the priests, the Brahmins who are muttering the holiest of their *mantras*, the mysterious sun-invocation from the Rig-Veda—the famous Gâyatrî[1]—the priestesses, the

[1] It has been translated as follows:—"Let us adore the light of the Divine Sun. May it enlighten our minds." But in Hindu ritual a mystic significance has been attached to it as a *mantram* especially addressed to the Supreme Soul—Brahman. It is said that Brahmâ composed it and taught it to Indra, who taught it to Yama; Yama taught it to Shiva, who taught it to the Brahmins.

women whose *saris* repeat the colours of the dawn, fast fading now in the white light of day; the votive-offerings, the golden marigolds and rose-petals which are piled in baskets on the ghât steps, and float on the surface of the water.

But this is not the simple nature-worship of the early Aryan patriarchs, who three thousand years before recited their odes to Ushas, Surya, and Agni, lighted the sacred fire, and pressed the *soma*-juice on the banks of the Ganges. The smoke which ascends from Manikarnika Ghât is from the funeral pyres of dead Hindus. Two vultures in mid-stream are fighting over a carcass, perhaps the corpse of a sannyâsî which was thrown into the river a few days ago. It is Shiva, the Destroyer, the principle of Life in Death, who is now worshipped at Benares, under his symbol of the serpent and his phallic emblem, which appears in every temple and is piled in thousands in the shrines along the ghâts. And, truly, the whole scene presents a wonderful picture of the Hindu conception of the Divine essence: on every ghât an ever-changing multitude of men, women, and children; cattle sunning themselves on the steps, goats and monkeys climbing on the cornices of the temples; kites, pigeons, and parrots flying overhead—but, here, a corpse laid down by the water's edge; a young woman distracted, her head buried in her mother's lap, and three sad-eyed grand-dames, wrapped in widows' *saris*, gazing dreamily into space. Yonder, the funeral pyres where three more corpses are already burning.

If we observe the bathers more closely, we can see that, besides the ordinary ablutions, many of them are performing mysterious rites of different kinds. Some are saluting the sun by splashing water towards it with both hands, or pouring out water from vessels of various shape, of brass, copper, and of a kind of cocoanut shell. Others take up water in the palms of their hands and pour it over the top of their heads. This is to free the body from the pollution of sins. Again, others, wearing the sacred *upavita*, or Brahminical thread, will first change it from the right shoulder to the left, and then, taking up water in the right hand, they will let it fall over their extended fingers. Next, placing the thread on their necks, they will let the water run over the side of the hand, between the thumb and bent forefinger. These are rites addressed to the Devas and Rishis—the gods and the sages. Many are counting the beads of their rosaries, muttering some mysterious formulary, others are rubbing their bodies with ashes from the sacrificial fire, or putting the symbol of Shiva or Vishnu on their foreheads. Here you will see a Brahmin performing what is known as "the exercise of breathing" (prânâyama). Stopping the right nostril with the thumb, he expels the breath through the left. Then he inhales through the left nostril, and compressing it inhales through the

A SANNYÂSI'S WATER-VESSEL

right. Finally he stops inspiration completely with thumb and forefinger, and holds his breath as long as he can. You will see him later on cover his right hand with his cloth, or thrust it into a red bag. He then begins to make symbolic signs with his fingers and thumb to represent the ten incarnations of Vishnu. The words he is muttering in undertones, lest the uninitiated or low-caste should overhear, are *mantras*, sacred texts and formulas, passages from the Vedas, the names or attributes of deities repeated in various ways; or invocations to the Supreme Being in his endless manifestations, prefixed by the mystic syllable AUM, representing the Hindu trinity — Brahmâ, the Creator, Vishnu, the Preserver, and Shiva, the Destroyer, or the three worlds—Earth, Air, and Heaven. All these complicated ceremonies form part of the Brahmin's *sandhya*, the form of prayer which he is enjoined to repeat three times daily—in the morning, at mid-day, and in the evening. But the *sandhya* is something more than prayer. It is a spiritual exercise which is believed to free the individual human soul from earthly contaminations, to place it in direct relation with the super-physical world, and to prepare it for the ultimate goal of all Hindu ritual—meditation. These rites and *mantras*, according to Hindu theories, are based on the science of the worlds invisible; but to attain the desired end they must be performed with absolute exactitude. Every *mantra*, every movement,

A SHIVAITE ROSARY

"He will sit like a living Buddha, motionless"

even the order and sequence of each ceremonial act, have their proper mystical significance. A wrong word, mispronunciation or false intonation, an error in the order or manner of the performance will vitiate the efficacy of the whole and bring misfortune on the performer. Hence the intense earnestness and absorption with which the bathers go through these ceremonies. Their usual curiosity at the sight of a European stranger is entirely suppressed; they seem not to see the passing boats or to heed the inquisitive traveller. Daily on the banks of the Ganges the pious Brahmin, who observes the strict rule of the twice-born caste, fulfils with the most scrupulous exactitude the prescribed order and detail of his *sandhya*, laid down by traditions jealously guarded through thousands of years. Then with mind and body thus prepared, folding his yellow robe about him, he will sit like a living Buddha motionless on the edge of the sacred river, with closed eyes and an expression of profound tranquillity on his face, absorbed in meditation on the Supreme Soul, Brahman, the Only Reality—THAT WHICH IS.

It is not to be supposed that every bather goes through the complicated ritual which I have just described, or that every Hindu on the banks of the Ganges takes the high spiritual stand-point of the philosophic Brahmin. Almost every sect and caste of Hinduism are represented among the thousands of worshippers, differing in race, language, and customs, who daily throng the ghâts. Many are simple, ignorant peasants, coming on a pilgrimage to the sacred city, who go through the traditional form of *sandhya* adopted by their caste, or only repeat a *mantra*, or mystic formula, prescribed for them by their Brahmin *gurus*, acting as their spiritual physicians. Others, again, are there in fulfilment of a vow, or to cleanse themselves by bathing from some ceremonial pollution. High-caste and low-caste, Brahmin and Sudra, bathe side by side, for the holy Ganges, descending from heaven and falling over Shiva's brow, not only effaces caste distinctions, but affords a panacea for most of the ills, bodily and spiritual, which afflict the distressed Hindu. The water is taken in brass and copper vessels for use in the endless ceremonies of the household, for sprinkling on holy shrines, or for drinking. It is carried away by pilgrims in sealed jars to their distant homes, for a few drops of the precious liquid on a dying man's lips have all the virtues of the sacred stream itself. Bathing in the Ganges is a part of many domestic ceremonies. You may observe a young couple, lately married, entering the water hand in hand, a corner of the bride's *sari* tied to the bridegroom's cloth; or perhaps a gray-haired pair, who thus celebrate an anniversary, or return thanks for recovery from illness—praying that in their next incarnations on earth they may be happily united once again.

Happy is the Hindu who dies in Benares, for he is transported at once to Shiva's Himalayan paradise, on Mount Kailâsa, north of Lake Mânasa, where the great three-eyed ascetic, seeing the past, the present, and the future, sits in profound meditation—the type of spiritual power gained by restraint of bodily passions. To win this easy passport to heaven, old men and women, who have left the world behind them, come to spend their last days within the boundaries

THE BURNING GHÂT

(From a photograph by Johnston & Hoffmann)

of Shiva's city, devoting themselves entirely to the prescribed observances of the Brahmin ritual. Some of the principal funeral rites take place on the banks of the Ganges. The nearest relatives of the deceased carry the body to the river, and place it by the water's edge, either near to the burning ghât, or close by the ghât where he or she would daily come to bathe. When the last offices of the dead have been performed by the relatives, the corpse is placed on the funeral pyre, prepared by the low-caste Doms at the burning ghât, who, however, are not allowed to touch any but the bodies of people of their own caste.

There are two exceptions to the ordinary rule of cremation of the dead. A *sannyâsî*, the Brahmin who, after passing through the stages of studentship and householdership, has renounced a worldly life and entered upon the strict ascetic rule of his religion, is thereby freed from the pollutions which infect the common clay, and his body after death is considered too holy to require the purification of the funeral pyre. The strangest sight of all to be seen along the ghâts is the sannyâsî's corpse, tenderly carried down by his disciples or other Brahmins of his sect, then posed like a bronze idol on the steps, garlanded and reverently saluted, while the temple musicians blow the sacred conch and beat the drums to announce that another human soul has finished the painful cycle of transmigration on earth, and is about to re-enter into union with the Absolute. The body, placed between two large flat stones, is afterwards removed to a boat and thrown into the river, opposite to the shrine where the sannyâsî had been accustomed to worship.

The other exception to the rule of cremation is in

the case of bodies of Hindus who have died of small-pox. According to the weird imaginings of Puranic Hinduism, they are supposed to become possessed by Sitala, the goddess of small-pox, one of the manifestations of the Destroyer, and the goddess would be offended if Agni, the god of Fire, drove her from her habitation.

It would be impossible to describe, or even to enumerate, all the rites and ceremonies which can be observed along the ghâts, changing according to the day, the month, or the occasion of the numerous Hindu festivals. The most beautiful of all the latter is the Diwâlî, or Feast of Lamps, in honour of Lakshmî, the goddess of Fortune, at the end of the month of Kartik (October–November). In the evening, when the short Eastern gloaming is merging into night, numbers of girls and young women, graceful as Greek nymphs in their many-coloured *saris*, come silently down to the ghâts bearing little earthen lamps, which they light and carefully set afloat. Then with eager faces they watch them carried away on the rippling surface of the water, still shimmering with opalescent tints from the last rays of the after-glow. For if a tiny wavelet should upset the frail craft, or if the light should flicker and go out, it bodes misfortune in the coming year. But if the light burns strong and well, till the lamp is borne far away by the current in mid-stream, happiness is in store for her who launched it on the waters. By the time the twilight fades there are hundreds of twinkling lights dotted over the river, as if holy Ganga had borrowed the stars from heaven, whence she came, to adorn her earthly robes. The buildings, platforms, and steps along the shore now gleam with rows of lamps which the pious elders have lighted for their worship. Our boat drifts slowly down the stream, through the fitful glimmer of Lakshmî's fragile fleet, which magnifies the lofty piles towering above the ghâts into some gigantic citadel, built by the Djinns of Eastern legends. Below the Observatory the lamps get fewer and fewer, and near Manikarnika the whole scene fades away, as the lurid glare of the funeral pyres flashes across the water, amidst the inky blackness of the burning ghât. Dark figures are crouching on the great smoke-begrimed piers which flank the ghât, and demoniacal forms appear moving to and fro between the flaming heaps. A horrid crackling noise arises from the burning wood. From the darkness up above comes the raucous note of a temple conch, and the booming of drums.

Presently a strangely familiar sound comes floating on the still night air, like a Gregorian chant with its slow and solemn cadence. In a distant monastery high above us the Brahmins are chanting the old sacrificial hymns, the Sâm-Ved, which the Aryan priests may have chanted here thirty centuries ago—still held so holy that it is sacrilege for our impure ears to listen. They are singing the praises of Rudra, the Mighty, the Terrible, lord of sacrifices, who has a thousand eyes, and carries a thousand quivers full of arrows of destruction.

CHAPTER VII

THE GHÂTS. ASI-SANGAM TO NEPÂLI GHÂT

The European traveller generally makes first acquaintance with the ghâts of the river at Dasâsamedh—the ghât of the Ten-Horse Sacrifice—to which the principal roads of the city converge. It is also an important point in the river traffic, for the boats bringing stone from the Chunar quarries, which have supplied Benares with building material from times immemorial, here discharge their cargoes. The popular legend which accounts for the name of the ghât probably refers to the time when the Brahmins were beginning to recover their authority in the city, on the decline of Buddhism. The story goes that all the gods had been expelled from Benares by Raja Divodâs, who had acquired extraordinary power by the practice of religious rites. Shiva, wishing to return to the city, invoked the aid of Brahmá, who transformed himself into an aged Brahmin, and sought an interview with the raja. The latter received him with much respect, and begged him to ask whatever he might desire. Brahmâ replied that the only favour he craved was that the raja would furnish the materials for the great horse-sacrifice.

Now this was one of the most complicated of the Brahminical sacrifices, requiring a perfect knowledge

DASÂSAMEDH GHÂT

(From a photograph by Johnston & Hoffmann)

of the divine science, and Brahmâ hoped that the raja might commit some trivial error, or omit some necessary material, and thus show his unfitness to rule over the holy city. Divodâs, however, was more than equal to the occasion, and supplied correct materials, not for one sacrifice only, but for ten. Brahmâ then performed the ten-horse sacrifice at this ghât, the virtue of which was so great that Dasâsamedh Ghât retains a special sanctity to this day. Finding his mission unsuccessful, Brahmâ thought it better to remain at Benares and leave to Shiva the task he himself had failed to accomplish. The wily raja was subsequently evicted by a trick played upon him by Ganêsha, the son of Shiva and god of Wisdom.

Such is the quaint legend by which the Brahmins account for this ghât being reckoned among the five places to be visited in the Panch-tirth, which is one of the religious ceremonies to be performed by Hindus who come to Benares. The European, however, will be more interested in the first view of the great amphitheatre of the ghâts—stretching from the little stream called Asi, on the north, to the river Barna, on the south;[1] in the wonderful picturesqueness of this approach to the river, the crowds of bathers, and the procession of men, women, and children coming to and from their ablutions. All will bring with them the brass or copper vessels used in the ceremonies of the bath. Some carry the sacred leaves, flowers, and other offerings necessary in the temple worship or *puja*.

For several months after the monsoon floods have

[1] The name of Benares is generally derived from a combination of the two words "Barna" and "Asi".

subsided, and the river has retreated to its normal bed, diggers are busy in removing the silt from the ghât steps, and in excavating the shrines which have been completely buried in the thick deposit. There are three such shrines at Dasâsamedh, which are yearly dug out of the river mud. The superstructure of two of them has completely disappeared. In the first there is a *lingam* with four heads on it, symbolizing the idea of Mahâdeva, or Shiva as Ishwara, manifesting himself as the four gods—Brahmâ, Vishnu, Shiva, and Surya. In front are two sculptured bulls; the bull, or *Nandi*, being sacred to Shiva, and perhaps symbolic of the animal creation, as Nandi is considered to be the guardian of all quadrupeds. In esoteric Hinduism Shiva's bull is sometimes regarded as representing the *Dharma*, "the Faith", or the whole duty of the Hindu.

The next shrine seems to be of great antiquity, as its foundations go deep below the present slope of the ghâts. It may be the remains of an ancient temple of Surya, the Vedic sun-god, who is still worshipped in many parts of India, though generally he has become merged into Vishnu, whose attributes are very similar to his. There are now three sculptured stones inserted in the face of one of the walls, which are all that remain of the temple. The centre one represents Kârttikeya, the war-god, the son of Shiva, whose birth has been celebrated by the great Sanskrit poet, Kâlidâs. He is represented with six heads and twelve arms, riding on a peacock. On the right is a figure of Ganêsha, a grotesque divinity with a fat belly and an elephant's head. He is another son of Shiva, lord of the Ganas, the nine classes of inferior deities which attend upon his father. As god of wisdom he may possibly symbolize the Brahminical philosophy which brought into one system the primitive faiths of the subject non-Aryan races.

At the end of December, when the annual excavations will have been nearly completed, there will be seen a deep hole in front of this shrine, at the bottom of which is an ancient suttee stone, marking the place where a Hindu widow sacrificed herself on the funeral pyre of her husband. There are many of these scattered up and down the ghâts, especially at the different burning-places. It is difficult to realize that the practice of self-immolation, which was often forced upon the unfortunate widows by their relatives, was only made illegal in British territory in 1829, and continued with the sanction of the law in the independent native states for some time afterwards. In 1839, at the funeral of Ranjit Singh, Maharaja of Lahore, his four wives and seven slave-girls sacrificed themselves on his pyre.

In the month of Kartik (October–November), on the last day of the Kâlî-puja, there is an imposing ceremony at Dasâsamedh Ghât, when the images of the goddess are thrown into the river, after completion of the traditional worship. The principal procession starts from the house of Babu Kâlidâs Mitra, whose family for several hundred years has taken the leading part in the ceremony. The image of the goddess, a repulsive black figure with natural hair, like a child's doll, and a protruding tongue, representing Kâlî trampling on the prostrate figure of Mahâ-Kâl (Time), is taken from her shrine in the house and placed in a state palanquin. Then, accompanied by bands of music and a procession of elephants, camels, and carriages, it is conducted with much state to the ghât. The idol is here lifted from the palanquin, the jewels which adorn it are removed, and a few locks of the hair reverently cut off. Then about sunset, the worship for the year being over, it is handed over to two swimmers, who take the idol and sink it in mid-stream. Many other images belonging to other households are brought to this ghât at the same time, placed upon boats, and then thrown into the river. The whole ceremony is strikingly picturesque, and if the abstract ideas personified by Kâlî were clothed in a more artistic garb, it might suggest a festival of pagan Rome on the banks of the Tiber. The Dîwâlî, the beautiful festival of Lakshmî, the goddess of Fortune, takes place the same evening.

The practice of throwing away the images or symbols of a deity is not associated only with Kâlî worship, but is a universal practice when they are made of clay or other base material. Brass, bronze, copper, and the precious metals are used when the idols are kept for regular daily worship, or in the temples.

Kâlî, in esoteric Hinduism, represents that stage in the evolution of the universe from the Supreme Brahman, before even the gods were created, as described in the Rig-Veda: "When darkness was hidden in darkness, undistinguished, like one mass of water". The Mahânirvan Tantra says: "As all colours, white, yellow, and others, are absorbed in black, so all the elements are in the end absorbed in Kâlî; and as the absence of all colours is black, so Kâlî is represented black in order to teach the worshipper that the goddess is without substance and without qualities (*gunas*)". Kâlî in this aspect, therefore, is regarded as the benignant mother of the universe, and her name means "darkness", or "chaos". But, like Shiva, she has a destructive aspect, in which her name is taken to mean Kâl-hârani, "she who destroys Time", implying that it is Kâlî as the wife, or *sakti*, of Mahâkâl, "Time", who, at the end of each cycle of time, a day and night of Brahmâ, called a *kalpa*, and reckoned at 8,640,000,000 years, destroys the whole of Brahmâ's creation and all the gods. For this reason she is represented as trampling on her own husband, Mahâkâl, one of the aspects of Shiva.

Immediately to the south of Dasâsamedh Ghât is Sitala Ghât, so called from the temple of Sitala, the goddess of small-pox, one of the popular Hindu deities which are regarded as manifestations of the Destroyer. It is a small box-like structure, without any attempt at architectural embellishment, but it is, nevertheless, much frequented by worshippers anxious to avert the evil influence of the goddess. She is represented by an old piece of stone-carving from which almost every detail has been obliterated, placed on a repoussé shrine of modern workmanship. Stone emblems of Shiva occupy prominent positions on the floor. An ancient carving of Shiva and Parvati, his wife, stands in a corner of the shrine at the back, but is worshipped as Vishnu and Lakshmî, the Brahmin priests being very indifferent to nice archæological distinctions. In the early morning a constant stream of worshippers is passing in and out, sprinkling the shrine of Sitala, and Shiva's emblems, with Ganges

THE TEMPLE OF SITALA

water, and throwing the sacrificial flowers and oblations of rice. Some will wet their fingers with the water which has been poured over the goddess and apply them to their foreheads and eyes. Those who have recovered from an attack of small-pox take a bath in this water.

Continuing along the ghâts towards the south, we shall pass the Munshi Ghât, a massive pile, with a colossal basement to provide for the rising of the river in flood-time, built by a Munshi, or minister of a former Raja of Vizianagram. A part of this ghât is one of the few places now reserved for Muhammadan bathers in the city, which Aurangzîb arrogantly re-named Muhammadâbâd, after levelling its Hindu temples to the ground. Farther on is Râna Ghât, where the Râna of Udaipur has built a palace. Many of the buildings along the ghâts here and else-where are occupied by Brahmin sannyâsin, supported by allowances granted them by Hindu princes and noblemen. The Brahmin only attains to the full dignity of his Brahminhood, when, in accordance with the law of Manu, he renounces the world and becomes a sannyâsî. Then in orthodox Hindu society he is regarded, living or dead, with all the veneration due to a divine being. The houses in Benares where sannyâsin have died are pointed out as if the sanctity of a temple belonged to them. According to Manu, the life of a Brahmin is divided into four stages. First, the state of studentship; the second, the state of married life and of family duties; thirdly, the state of the ascetic, retiring from the world and devoting himself entirely to religious practices and meditation; and lastly, the state of the religious mendicant, or sannyâsî, when, after breaking his sacred thread, the symbol of his caste, and shaving his head, he is re-leased from the performance of rites and ceremonies, and prepares himself for the final absorption of his soul into the Absolute.

It is hardly necessary to say that the laws of Manu are not strictly observed in the present day. British rule and modern ideas are gradually breaking down

A SANSKRIT SCHOOL

the old social system and modifying the religious life of the Hindu. The Brahmins who now adopt a religious life, often devote themselves to teaching in Sanskrit schools, of which there are many in Benares. Just above Chausatti Ghât, on an open terrace, the yellow-robed sannyâsin, in their salmon-coloured robes, may be seen with their young pupils, studying the intricacies of Pânini, the celebrated Sanskrit grammarian, who is reverenced as one of the Hindu Rishis, or inspired sages.

There are, however, some sannyâsin at Benares who follow the strict rule of their caste, hoping to free their souls from earthly ties by meditation on the Supreme Being, or by Yogic practices. The latter are certain spiritual exercises, enjoined by the Yoga school of philosophy, through the performance of which it is believed that the human soul can be raised during lifetime into a super-terrestrial plane, and acquire supernatural knowledge. The practices of the fanatics of the Yoga school, who go through all kinds of fearful bodily tortures to attain this end, are too well known to need description, but among the exercises which are not performed in public, except in very special circumstances, is one by which, according to the sacred books of the Hindus, the Yogi, in a kind of trance, can overcome the law of gravity and remain suspended, or seated in the air, at a lower or higher altitude, according to the force of the Yogic power he may have acquired. Educated Indians of the present day consider these extraordinary attainments as beyond the reach of this materialistic age, but there are a few sannyâsin at Benares who pretend to possess them. I have never succeeded in persuading any of them to submit to a test which would satisfy scepticism; but in 1887, when presiding over the celebration of the Queen Victoria jubilee, at a remote village in the Kurnool district of Madras, I saw a performance by a Yogi, held in great respect in the neighbourhood, who as a special favour had consented to exhibit his powers in public to honour the occasion. He placed himself behind a curtain, and when it was drawn, the Yogi was seen, as if in a trance, apparently poised in the air, several feet above the ground, cross-legged and absolutely motionless. He remained in this position for perhaps fifteen minutes, when the curtain was again drawn in front of him.

A case is recorded in the *Asiatic Monthly Journal* for March, 1829, and referred to by Sir Monier Williams in his *Indian Wisdom*, in which a Brahmin created some excitement in Madras, and exhibited himself before the Governor, apparently poised in the air, for forty minutes. But neither did this Yogi, nor the one who honoured the Queen Victoria jubilee in a similar fashion, dispense with the screen, which to ordinary intelligences gives an unfortunate aspect of conjuring to the performance.

Proceeding up the river, the next ghât of interest is

CARVED SNAKES AT CHAUKI GHÂT

Chauki Ghât, where, under a fine old *pippal*-tree, there is a small shrine and a great number of old carved stones, some of snakes, twined together like Mercury's *caduceus*, with the *lingam* placed between. The worship of snakes, especially as emblems of the Earth Goddess, is one of the most ancient of Indian cults, and these stones, together with some fine figure-sculptures let into the upright face of the platform which surrounds the tree, are probably relics of the early Buddhist period.

The pippal (*ficus religiosa*) has been associated with the religious ceremonies of the Hindus from the earliest Vedic times. Its wood was used in the making of the drill which produced the sacred fire of Agni, and for various sacrificial vessels. Philosophers and holy men in all ages have chosen its leafy shade as a fit place for meditation. Among Buddhists it is especially venerated as the Bodhi tree —the tree of wisdom—under which their great leader obtained enlightenment. In popular imagination it is regarded as the Brahmin among trees. In southern India it is sometimes invested with the sacred cord of the Brahmins, and with the same ceremonies as used by them.[1] The banyan-tree, another kind of fig, is frequently seen growing next to the pippal, and receives almost equal veneration.

Beyond Chauki Ghât is the burning ghât of the southern part of the city. Close by it, in a stone cell raised high above the ghât, lives a sannyâsî of the Aghori sect, the name of which, meaning "horrible", sufficiently indicates their ideas. The Aghoris give an extreme interpretation to the Vedantic doctrine of the Universal Soul. As all things proceed from and are part of Brahman, nothing, they argue, is really impure, and they are prepared to prove the strength of their convictions by eating everything commonly considered abominable, even putrid corpses. It must be said, however, that the revolting practices com-

[1] Dubois, Vol. II, Beauchamp's edition, p. 660.

monly attributed to the Aghoris do not seem to be committed by the black-robed ascetic devoutly reading at this ghât, who bestows his blessing on the prying

AN AGHORI

tourist, but contemptuously refuses to accept any of the usual *bakshish.*

Near his cell is a suttee stone of unusually elaborate construction, on which is carved with much quaint grace and feeling a youthful couple who shared the funeral pyre together at this ghât. The husband has one arm affectionately clasped round the neck of his unfortunate bride.

Kedarnath Ghât, which is immediately above this burning ghât, is named after Shiva's shrine of Kedarnath, high up among the Himalayan glaciers, and one of the most sacred places of Hindu pilgrimage. Here there is nothing to suggest the grandeur of the Hima-

A SUTTEE STONE

layan snows, the noble deodars, "the tree of the gods", and the beauty of the wild flowers; only a plain temple crowns the lofty pile of steps, and a small reservoir of dirty water, alive with myriads of frogs. The latter goes by the name of Gauri-kund, the tank of Gauri—another name of Durgâ, the wife of Shiva—and is supposed to possess all sorts of healing virtues.

There is, however, plenty of human interest in the crowds of bathers, mostly Bengalis, who inhabit this quarter of the city. Behind, a picturesque street runs parallel with the river down to Dasâsamedh Ghât.

Some distance farther up the river, Shivâla Ghât and Fort present an imposing front to the river. The fort was the former residence of the Maharaja of Benares, and was occupied by Chêt Singh in the days of Warren Hastings. A yellow flag is flying above the trees within the northern enclosure of the old fort, proclaiming the presence of some Hindu ascetics. This is a *math*, or monastery, inhabited by some fifteen or twenty followers of Kapila, the reputed founder of the Sankhya school of philosophy, who is believed to have lived at Benares about B.C. 700. The spacious courtyard is bright with marigolds, and under the shade of some fine old fruit-trees the monks pass their time in quiet devotion. They will give visitors a friendly greeting, offering a handful of cardamoms, with excuses for their inability to show more lavish hospitality. At the time of my visit there was an old monk, spectacled, nearly blind, and stone-deaf, who was said to be 103 years old. Another venerable hermit seated on a leopard's skin had better use of his faculties, and claimed to be 150. He had known, he said, eight rajas, and remembered Chêt Singh and the days of Warren Hastings. They believed that Kapila, whose footprints were worshipped in a little shrine in the courtyard, was still living in an island at the mouth of the Ganges. They all deplored that the philosophy which once had so many followers was now considered out of date; and the worldliness of modern times had come into their quiet, recluse life, for on my leaving

"Another venerable hermit, seated on a leopard's skin"

they produced a printed form from the municipality demanding payment of the water-rate, and requested my help in mitigating the severity of the authorities towards their peaceful hermitage. The founder of the *math*, Lakhi Baba, perhaps one of the Dîwans of Chêt Singh, lies buried under a mango-tree at the entrance.

We will leave Shivâla Ghât and its fine old fort for a time, and proceed farther up the river. From Bachraj Ghât up to Asi Sangam the shooting of birds and catching of fish are forbidden out of respect for the feelings of the Jains, who have several temples along this part of the river. As with the Buddhists, the doctrine of the sacredness of all life is an important principle of the Jain faith.

Probably along this part of the ghâts we shall pass several rude, colossal mud figures of Bhîma, one of the Pândava brothers in the Mahâbhârata, stretched full length on the ground. The story which explains why Bhîma is worshipped for the last five days of the month of Kartik is as follows:—Bhîma was a man of enormous size and strength, and had a correspondingly prodigious appetite. Like a good Hindu, he wished to worship Krishna in the month of Kartik, but found the fasting so irksome that he begged Krishna to relax the rule in his favour. To accommodate the hungry giant, Krishna agreed that if Bhîma would fast for the last five days of the month he should be granted the merit which attached to the whole month's fasting, and, further, as a special mark of favour, that those who worshipped Bhîma the last five days of Kartik should gain the same merit.

In this month there will also be many high pedestals

of clay, on which are placed for worship sprigs of the sacred basil (*ocymum sanctum*), or tulasi, Vishnu's plant, as it is Vishnu in his Krishna incarnation who is specially worshipped in Kartik. The tulasi was, says the legend, a woman of Brindâban, who loved Krishna so passionately, that at last she threw herself into the flames of a suttee's pyre. Krishna then transformed her into the sacred plant, and directed that it should always be worshipped as part of his own puja. At Asi Sangam we reach the southern limit of Benares. From the other side of the little stream from which the ghât takes its name, the Panch-kôsi road begins to wind through the corn-fields.

We will now return downstream to Man Mandil Ghât, just below Dasâsamedh. The great building fronting this ghât is the oldest of the palaces in Benares, having been built by Man Singh, Raja of Amber, and ancestor of the present Maharaja of Jaipur, about the year 1600 A.D. It was a very fine specimen of the architecture of that period, and the beautiful stone balcony, which is the chief feature of the present façade, is part of the original work. Unfortunately, the greater part of the building fell into ruin, and about the middle of the last century was restored with brick and plaster of a very inferior style. A picture by Daniell, now in the rooms of the Asiatic Society, Calcutta, shows the original façade as built by Man Singh.

The palace was converted into an observatory in 1693 by the great Hindu astronomer, Raja Jai Singh, a descendant of Man Singh, who was employed by the Mogul emperor, Muhammad Shah, to correct the

SHIVÂLA GHÂT

By permission of H.H. the Maharaja of Benares

calendar, which had become very erroneous owing to the inaccuracy of the then existing tables. He built

BALCONY OF MAN SINGH'S OBSERVATORY

four other observatories, at Delhi, Muttra, Ujjain, and at Jaipur. The latter city was one of the bold designs planned and carried out by this remarkable man. A long stone staircase outside the observatory, on the southern side, leads up to a single chamber recessed in the wall, where a number of Brahmins may be seen daily going through a series of gymnastic exercises very similar to the forms of physical culture now so much in vogue in Europe. The approach to the interior of the observatory is through a lane on the opposite side. Within there is not much of the original building left, except the great astronomical instruments invented by Jai Singh. They are not now in working order.

Close by the approach to the observatory is a little temple known as Dalbhyeswar. Shiva's emblem is placed low down in a cistern within the shrine, and in times of drought water is poured in, so that the temple is filled up to the threshold, with the idea that it will act as a charm to compel rain. Near this is another small temple, dedicated to Shiva as lord of Soma, the moon—the shining bowl from which the Vedic gods and the Pitris drunk their nectar of Soma-juice, and the place of all health-giving and healing herbs. This temple is much resorted to on account of the curative powers still attributed to the moon.

The next ghât downstream is Nepâli Ghât, where, recessed in the stone embankment, and completely covered by the river in the rainy season, is a pretty little shrine of Ganga, the Ganges, represented as a female figure seated on a crocodile. Above it a staircase leads to the Nepalese temple, a very picturesque building, half-hidden by magnificent tamarind and pippal trees. It is built chiefly of wood and brick; the double-storied roof, with great projecting eaves supported by brackets, is characteristic of the architecture of Nepal and of other sub-Himalayan districts.

THE NEPALESE TEMPLE

The rich carvings with which the wood-work is ornamented are disfigured with many gross obscenities not usually found in Shivaite temples in northern India.

THE SHRINE OF GANGA

CHAPTER VIII

THE GHÂTS—FROM MANIKARNIKA TO BARNA SANGAM

At Manikarnika we reach the central point of the ghâts—the very pivot of the religious life of Benares. There is perhaps no more extraordinary sight in the whole world than this ghât presents any morning in the month of Kartik, or at the time of a great Hindu festival. Shrines innumerable, cut in the stone piers and terraces which project into the stream; temples at the water's edge, half-sunk in the stream; temples on the ghât steps; the five-spired temples of Durgâ crowning the high ridge above. The burning ghât, black with the smoke of funeral pyres; corpses laid out by the river on their rough biers of bamboo. A few yards away, the women's bathing ghât, glowing like a flower-garden with the colours of their *saris.* Further on, a forest of palm-leaf umbrellas, where men in crowds are bathing, praying, muttering their *mantras*, marking their bodies with the signs of Shiva or Vishnu, or sitting self-absorbed as if the world and its illusions had vanished from their eyes. Pilgrims from every quarter of India, carrying their bundles with them, are arriving at the sacred well, brought there by the Ganga-putras to begin their round of devotions, which is often preceded by clamorous disputes for the fees their spiritual preceptors demand.

"Groups of women . . . are performing puja"

Groups of women sitting in circles on the level ground above the ghât steps are performing puja, perhaps that of Prithivî, the earth goddess, or of the holy Ganges, some old grandmother making symbolic figures of clay and directing the ceremonies. Devout widows, their *saris* stamped with sacred texts, will pause on their way home to watch them and sprinkle flowers and Ganges water upon the charmed circle. Others are making purchases of toys and sweetmeat vessels, which are piled in glittering heaps close by. A lordly bull comes pacing slowly through the crowds, snatching as he passes at garlands of marigolds worn by men and girls, and mumbling the rose-petals strewn on the wayside shrines and suttee-stones. Pigeons are fluttering overhead, goats clambering on the cornices of the buildings. Thin vaporous clouds of smoke rise from the funeral pyres. The slanting rays of the morning sun cast long shadows across the ghât, and diffuse a rosy light over the whole picture. (See page 195.)

To the Hindu pilgrim the great attraction of Manikarnika is the well, the origin of which is given in the Kâsî - Khanda, the legendary history of Benares. Vishnu, it is said, dug the well with his discus, and filled it with the perspiration from his own body. He then went to the north side of it and began to practise austerities. While he was thus engaged, the god Mahâdeva came and looked into the well. Seeing in it the radiance of a hundred million of suns, he was so enchanted that he began praising Vishnu loudly, and declared that he would give him anything he might ask. Vishnu, much gratified, replied that he only desired that Mahâdeva should always live there with him. Mahâdeva was so pleased with the compliment that his whole body shook with delight, and an ornament called Manikarnika fell from his ear into the well. He then declared that the well should henceforth be known by that name, and that it should be the first and most efficacious of all the places of pilgrimage—Benares.

There are several other popular legends accounting for the name of the well, one of which is that Mahâdeva and his wife, Parvati, were seated by the well, when a jewel fell from Parvati's ear into the water, and Mahâdeva gave the well the name of the ornament, Manikarnika.

Another object of devotion at this ghât is the *charan-pâdukâ*, a marble slab set into the ground, and carved with the figures of two footprints on which mystic signs are engraved. Almost every saint or divinity in Hinduism is supposed to have left visible footprints on earth, and these indicate the place where Vishnu is believed to have alighted before he began to practise ascetic rites and to worship Shiva as Mahâdeva, or Ishwara, at this ghât. The *charan-pâdukâ* is often made in silver or gold, and worn as a charm by Hindus.

Scindhia Ghât is named after a Hindu nobleman of Gwalior, whose widow, Baija Bai, in the early part of last century, commenced to build here a palace and bathing ghât. Before the basement had been raised many feet, the tremendous weight of the massive masonry caused a landslip, which made the whole fabric topple over, so that the work had to be abandoned. The unfinished façade and the ghât steps still remain—huge blocks of solid stone-work, thrown about

"Like a painted frieze from Pompeii or the decoration of an antique vase"

in picturesque confusion, as if an earthquake had torn them from their foundations. The warm tints of the Chunar stone, lighted by the morning sun, make a delightful colour-contrast for the bright *saris* of the women, as they pass in procession along the narrow path in front of the great corner piers, like a painted

SCINDHIA GHÂT

frieze from Pompeii, or the decoration of an antique vase.

This ghât is a favourite camping-ground for the wandering *Sâdhus*, or mendicant religious devotees, who travel throughout India from one place of pilgrimage to another, subsisting on the alms of the people. They are the modern representatives of the Bhiksus of ancient times, and like them are recruited from all classes of Hindus. There is this difference, however, between them and their prototypes, that a very large proportion of *Sâdhus* become devotees more from want of other means of livelihood, or from the attractions of a life which commands universal respect among Indian people, than from the promptings of a deep religious feeling. The decay of the old village handicrafts, largely due to want of proper technical instruction, has greatly helped to swell their numbers. It has been estimated that there are about five millions of them in India, of whom about seventy-five per cent are wholly illiterate.

It is a strange and sad sight, an encampment of these wild-looking mendicants, sometimes accompanied by small children, who, like themselves, are smeared with ashes, and observe all the forms of the sect to which they are attached. There are many different sects of *Sâdhus*, distinguished by the mark on their foreheads and by the symbols they carry with them. Shivaite devotees are generally indicated by three horizontal lines across the forehead, drawn with sacred ashes. They wear round their necks the rosary of rudra berries, and carry with them some of the emblems of Shiva, such as a *lingam*, a human skull, a *trisula* or trident, a drum, and perhaps a tiger's skin. The sectarial marks of the followers of Vishnu are nearly all perpendicular in direction, or converging towards the root of the nose, over which there is generally a central line or dot. Their rosary is made of beads, or rough sections of the stem of the tulasi plant, and they carry about with them the sacred symbols of Vishnu, the *salagram* stone, the white conch shell, and the discus, the emblem of the sun.

The *Sâdhus* mostly spend their time wandering from

AN ENCAMPMENT OF SÂDHUS

monastery to monastery, and from shrine to shrine—through the country where Râma and Sîtâ wandered in their exile, the places where Krishna was born, where he passed his childhood, sported with Radha and the milkmaids, and where he slew the demons which oppressed mankind. They will visit the battle-field of the Mahâbhârata, and places made sacred by the Pândava heroes, holy shrines in every part of India, and even penetrate beyond, into Baluchistan, Afghanistan, and Tibet. The armlets and necklets they wear are tokens of the pilgrimages they have made—a white conch-shell indicates the great temple of Râmêswaram in the extreme south; armlets of iron, brass, and copper, the three Himalayan shrines of Pasupatinath, Kedarnath, and Badrinath.

The *Sâdhus* who come in contact with Europeans do not generally give an impression of earnestness or piety. They are not above a certain vanity in the correctness of their peculiar toilet, which they perform punctiliously with the aid of a mirror, and are evidently flattered by the interest they excite. They are very ostentatious in the performance of their religious duties while they are conscious of being observed, but are much addicted to intoxicating drugs, and have not a high reputation for morality or respect for the law.

But there are undoubtedly many *Sâdhus* who, besides being learned in the ordinary sense, have the breadth of culture which extensive travelling has given them, and live up to the Indian ideal of a holy life. Sometimes they will devote themselves to collecting money for a religious purpose, such as for the repair or building of a temple. A great deal of the real Indian art which is unnoticed by Europeans and ignored by the official administration is kept alive in this way. The faith of the genuine *Sâdhu* often shows itself in extreme fanaticism. It is not an uncommon event for one of them, in a state of religious ecstasy, to throw himself into the sacred lake of Pushkar, near Ajmere, to be devoured by the crocodiles, or perhaps jump from a Himalayan precipice. The most tragic end of all, is of those who set themselves to follow that journey of the great Pândava heroes, when, tired of life, they started forth towards Indra's paradise beyond the Himalayan snows, dropping one by one on the way, until Yudhishthira alone was received at the gates of *Swarga*. Even so the *Sâdhu*, following Yudhishthira's footsteps, will start forth on that last great pilgrimage, toiling on and on until he reaches those mighty snow-clad peaks, and is lost to mortal sight for ever.

We will continue on our way down the ghâts, passing Baji Rao Ghât and Ghôsla Ghât, where there are two imposing buildings built by the owner, the Raja of Nagpur. Next we get to Ram Ghât, one of the long stretches of the river bank which are not lined with masonry steps. Wherever these occur we shall probably see some of the low-caste dôms digging in the mud for treasure, in the shape of ornaments, small idols, or sacrificial vessels, which are afterwards brought to the bazaar for sale. Ram Ghât is named in honour of the hero of the Râmâyana, who is worshipped as one of the ten incarnations of Vishnu.

Here a follower of Vishnu has established himself with a shrine containing a small museum of brass and copper images, odd stones and shells, and symbols of the deity. Next to him, in front of a small stone

THE BUILDINGS AT GHÔSLA GHÂT

temple, is one of those colossal mud figures of Bhîma, which have been alluded to previously. This one, however, is noticeable, as the artist takes unusual pride and care in the execution of it. It is amusing to observe the figure as it is gradually built up every year from about the first week in November until the whole is completed. The head alone is first carefully finished on the stone terrace in front of the temple, and, being perfectly erect, the observer might imagine that the sculptor's task was finished. The next day, however, a sloping bank of clay is heaped up in front of

THE HEAD OF BHIMA

the terrace, and the body and legs of this extraordinary figure begin to appear. The right arm is detached from the ground, and holds a wooden club, Bhîma's favourite weapon. A further touch of realism is given by the painting of the face, including an elegant moustache and the sectarial mark of Vaishnavite.

The figure remains in all its grotesqueness, with eyes staring out over the Ganges, until the monsoon flood rises and sweeps it entirely away.

Farther on is Chôr Ghât, the ghât of the Thief. There is a narrow staircase here by which access to the city can be gained without using any of the main

BHÎMA COMPLETED

thoroughfares. Tradition says that a noted thief used to come by this staircase when he wished to bathe in the Ganges unobserved. Close by this ghât is the fragment of a stone column, now worshipped as a *lingam*, which is probably one of the lâts, or columns, erected by Asoka or some other Buddhist sovereign, and inscribed with proclamations of the Buddhist faith. There is another of these, also worshipped as a *lingam*, called Lât Bhairo, in the northern quarter of the city, close to a large tank and other ancient remains.

Panchganga, or the ghât of the five sacred rivers, is so called from the five colossal flights of steps which lead up to the city from this point. Great blocks of picturesque buildings, flanking and overarching the steps, rise in tiers, one behind the other, until, at the summit of the high ridge which overlooks the river, Aurangzîb's mosque with its lofty minarets forms a landmark visible for miles around, and perpetuates the intolerant zeal of the great Muhammadan iconoclast. Here stood formerly a great temple of Shiva, which Aurangzîb destroyed, and perhaps in ancient times that one which Hiuen Thsang described, made of stone skilfully carved and of richly-painted wood, containing a brazen statue of Mahâdeva, a hundred feet high, "grave and majestic, filling the spectator with awe, and seeming as it were indeed alive". The five flights of steps would then appropriately symbolize the five sacred rivers flowing from the Himalayan heights, where Shiva's paradise is placed.

Panchganga Ghât is one of the five places of pilgrimage in Benares, and on the occasion of a Hindu festival the scene is almost as striking as at Manikarnika. In the month of Kartik the edge of the ghât is lined with a forest of bamboo poles, from which Chinese lanterns are suspended, placed there by the bathers, so that when the moon is on the wane the Pitris, the Fathers who dwell above in Pitriloka, may not be left in darkness. It is a pretty custom, too, that which the women observe on the full-moon night of the same month, when, after a bath at Panchganga, they place some sweetmeats in the moonlight, believing

LAMPS FOR THE PITRIS

that the falling dews will sprinkle them with *amrita*, the heavenly nectar with which King Soma refreshes gods, the Pitris, and men.

At the corner of one of the flights of steps are three remarkable stone lamp-stands, cone-shaped and fitted from top to bottom with numberless bracket oil-receptacles. When these are lighted up at the Dîwâlî, or other great Hindu festival, they appear like blazing fir-cones or cypress-trees, and suggest Saracenic rather than Hindu origin.

Probably they were made for the service of the mosque, and appropriated by the Hindus on the decline of Muhammadan rule. The mosque itself has no special interest, except for its historical associations, and were it not for its splendidly-chosen situation it would command no special attention; but it is worth while to climb the great pyramid of steps in order to see the little piazza in front of the mosque, which overlooks the river.

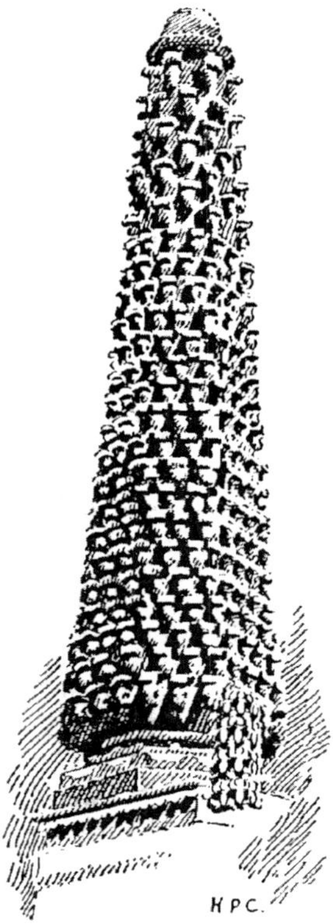

LAMP-STAND AT PANCHGANGA

It is like any piazza in Italy or Spain, but it gives an excellent coign of vantage where, after the time of the morning *sandhya*, one can observe the crowd returning from the river, take notes, or admire the groups which arrange themselves continually in all sorts of suggestive *tableaux vivants*. Here are three old women, who pause to barter with a seller of pots and pans, unconsciously posing themselves with their classic drapery like the Fates, or the Weird Sisters (p. 153). There is a shrine built round a *pippal*-tree, round which a procession of worshippers is constantly passing, sprinkling it with water of the sacred river. Later on, when the crowd is smaller, one notices a

"Three old women, who pause to barter with a seller of pots and pans, unconsciously posing themselves with their classic drapery like the Fates, or the Weird Sisters" (page 152)

Sâdhu, who at first sight seems to be inflicting upon himself a terrible penance. He is reclining on a low wooden bed, which, by way of a mattress, is studded all over with long iron spikes. On closer observation, however, it will be found that he has been careful to provide himself with a cushion for his back; the spikes are blunt, and so close together that probably they have never caused him very great inconvenience. He may impress the simple-minded pilgrim with an appearance of frightful austerity, but to the ordinary observer he presents rather an idyll of peace and self-satisfaction, as he reclines at ease in the sunshine, puffing occasionally at the *chillum* by his side and reading a pocket edition of the Bhagavad Gîta.

As a contrast to this innocent imposture, there is a young Vaishnavite nun worshipping in a primitive shrine close by, who seems to be an example of that simple piety which is often found among Indian women. The by-standers say that she has followed a religious life since childhood, and her modest demeanour and absence of affectation speak for her sincerity. She is wholly absorbed in reading the sacred books, and takes not the least notice either of the by-standers or of the camera which is levelled at her (p. 157).

Beyond Panchganga there is not much of interest until we get to Gâî Ghât. A colossal statue of the sacred cow, carved with much monumental dignity, here holds the place of honour on the ghât steps. Grouped in front of it you may often see statuesque women like nymphs or nereids, who, as they are bathing or robing themselves, take attitudes of perfect classic grace with an unconscious ease no artist's model could ever imitate. One could go on day after day along the ghâts through this wonderful panorama of Indian life, every day observing new customs and ceremonies, seeing new types of race, fresh *motifs* for

PALHVAD GHÂT

the painter or sculptor, different scenes in the drama of human existence—for Benares is the microcosm of all India.

After Gâî Ghât is Palhvad Ghât, another great flight

A VAISHNAVITE NUN READING THE RÂMÂYANA

of steps leading up to a group of little shrines sheltered by some splendid *pippal* trees. The end of the ghâts on the northern side of Benares is reached at Barna Sangam, where the river Barna joins the Ganges. This is one of the five sacred places of pilgrimage, and a bath in the meeting waters is held to be of special virtue in cleansing from all sin. The high ridge on which four temples are placed commands a fine view of the Ganges valley.

CHAPTER IX

THE TEMPLES AND SACRED WELLS

Hindus recognize three classes of deities, or three different aspects of divine worship. First, the patron deity of the village community, called *gramya deva.* The images or symbols of these are placed under a sacred tree outside the villages. Next is the household god, or the god which is regarded by each family as its special protector. Thirdly, the *ishta deva*—the personal god, or the god whom the *guru,* the spiritual adviser of each individual, appoints as his or her patron deity, after consultation of the person's horoscope.

Outside the Brahmin caste, the expenses attendant on the proper conduct of Hindu ritual make it impossible for any but those who have means to keep up the worship of their patron deity within the house, for only Brahmins, or those who claim the right of exercising priestly functions, can perform the appropriate ceremonies. The full performance of household worship is most complicated and expensive. The images or symbols used in daily worship are often made of clay, and these are made by the worshippers themselves and always thrown away directly the *pûjâ* is finished. But when an idol of stone or of metal is purchased for the house or temple the first ceremonial is a kind of consecration, called *prân prahtishta*, "life giving", performed by a Brahmin, who is supposed thereby to cause the divine essence to come and reside in the idol. Thereafter it is regarded as a being endowed with life and feeling, and in the worship in the temple, or in the household, daily, monthly, or yearly, as the case may be, it is washed and dressed, garlanded, offered food, drink, betel-leaf and areca-nut, and money, in sixteen prescribed ceremonies accompanied by the chanting of *mantras*.

THE SALAGRAM STONE

This is part of the regular worship, but there is practically no limit to the attentions which the devout Hindu will pay to his idol. In the hot weather it will be fanned to prevent flies and mosquitoes from annoying it, and bathed to keep it cool. In the cold weather it will be dressed in warm clothes. If the idol represents a masculine deity, it will be married with great pomp and ceremony to its reputed consort of the other sex. A marriage ceremony is a very popular form of religious devotion; failing a god and goddess, a sacred bird or animal, or even inanimate objects, such as the tulasi plant and the salagram stone, will serve as the make-believe bride and bridegroom. In response to these attentions the patron deity is expected to bestow corresponding worldly favours on the worshipper, otherwise the latter will sometimes visit his anger on his deity's image with all kinds of abuse and indignity.

Such is the contrast between the high philosophy of Hinduism and the ritual countenanced by its priestly exponents.

The ordinary Hindu, who has not the means or time for regular household worship, has to be content with hiring a Brahmin occasionally to recite a part of the sacred writings, and with visits to the temple on festival days, or when his leisure permits.

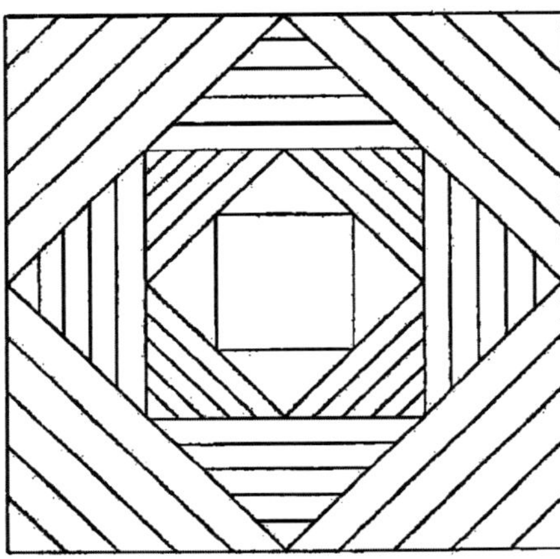

PLAN OF HINDU ROOFING

I have noticed before that though Benares is one of the most picturesque cities in India, it possesses hardly a single temple of first-rate architectural merit. The fifteen hundred or more temples it contains are small and nearly all of one type, with very little variation. The cell containing the image or sacred emblem is square, generally with an opening on all four sides, and surmounted by the tall curvilinear and multiform *sikra* or spire, already described (see p. 44) In front of this, and connected with it, is a larger colonnaded porch, which is roofed either by a dome or by

THE TEMPLE OF DURGÂ, OR "MONKEY TEMPLE"

Z

the more ancient and characteristic Indian method of building squares within squares, by filling in the corners of each square successively with superimposed horizontal layers or slabs of stone, as explained in the diagram. Surrounding the temple is a court or quadrangle enclosed by four walls, or by cloisters which contain subsidiary shrines, or accommodation for the priests.

The temple of Durgâ, the so-called Monkey Temple, is a good illustration of the type of a Benares temple, for being in the suburbs and not restricted by want of space, it is larger and more complete than most of the temples in the city. In front of the temple the *vahan*, on which the goddess rides, occupies a conspicuous position on a high pedestal somewhat suggestive of the famous column of St. Mark's Square at Venice. Sacrifices of goats are frequently offered at a stake close by. The goats are decapitated at one stroke of the knife, and the blood offered to the goddess, but the bodies are generally taken away by the sacrificers. The object of the sacrifice is various: sometimes to appease the goddess in a case of sickness, sometimes to invoke her aid when the sacrificer is out of employment. Often it is simply to provide a meal for Hindus who are not allowed to eat flesh, except that of animals offered in sacrifice.

The lion symbol is also painted on either side of the entrance, and appears again sculptured in stone on each side of the doorway within. The temple being one of the sights of the tourist, you are invited to purchase food for the monkeys, which climb nimbly down in crowds from the neighbouring roofs and trees, and scramble with all the vivacity of monkeyhood for the handfuls of grain and sweetmeats thrown to them. Though it is not Hanuman, the monkey god and the ally of Râma in his fight with Râvana, who is worshipped in the temple, the monkeys are found by the Brahmin attendants to be a successful draw for the *bakshish* of tourists. The cell where the image of Durgâ is placed was built by a Bengali Rânî at the end of the eighteenth century. The pillared porch in front dates from about the middle of the nineteenth. They are both fair specimens of modern Hindu temple architecture and decoration.

The image of Durgâ in this temple is an insignificant doll-like figure of no artistic merit. The illustration here given is from a fine stone bas-relief at Chamba[1], representing Durgâ, at the command of Shiva, destroying the Asuras, or demons who were usurping the authority of the gods and oppressing humanity. The face is unfortunately mutilated. Lying at her feet is the dead body of Mahisha, an Asura in the form of a buffalo, whom she slew.

Durgâ is one of the wives, or *saktis*, of Shiva. Her aspect is fair and shining, as her original name Gaurî signifies. She appears to be especially related to Shiva in his manifestation as god of the Himalayas, and to represent the destructive forces of creation, while Kâlî, whose images are always black, is the Earth-mother and the universal destroyer of Time, and the Cosmos. In every country the highest mountains have always been associated with the religious ideas of the people. The benignant and ferocious aspects of Indian mountain deities are doubtless but the impression on the Indian mind of the two aspects of those natural

[1] From a photograph by Dr. Vogel, Architectural Surveyor of the Punjab.

forces which are displayed in all their grandeur in the Himalayan regions. The fairy, snow-clad peaks, glorious in the sunshine, and full of solemn mystery

DURGÂ

by moonlight, pouring out from their violet depths the precious streams which fertilize the earth, are Umâ and Parvatî, kindly goddesses of light and beauty, and Shiva, the bountiful, moon-crested, blue-throated.

resplendent lord of bliss. Shrouded in fearful thunder-clouds, torn by furious winds and raging torrents, their mighty sides heaving with earthquakes and scarred with landslides which bring sudden and awful destruction on man and beast—they become Rudra "the Roarer", Ugra "the fierce", Shiva "the terrible destroyer", and Durgâ "the inaccessible", Raktadantî "the bloody-toothed".

Durgâ is especially appealed to for victory in war. She was the patron deity of Râvana, the demon-king of Ceylon, but Râma succeeded at last in bringing her over to his side, and thus overthrew his powerful foe. Probably she is one of the aboriginal deities adopted by the Aryans. As a fighting goddess she has a great reputation for destroying demons. Her chief exploit was the defeat of an Asura, called Durg, who had acquired extraordinary power by the practice of penances, and used it to bring the gods into subjection and to destroy religion on earth. To celebrate her victory she changed her name from Gaurî, "the shining one", to Durgâ. In one of the corners of the quadrangle in this Durgâ temple is a shrine of Kâlî. The idol, as is frequently the case in Benares temples, is nothing but a metal mask and a collection of gaudy draperies. These masks, however, are often fine pieces of repoussé work. An idol is sometimes provided with a series of masks with different expressions, to represent the different manifestations of the deity. An illustration is given here of a mask of Shiva, in gilt copper, from a temple in Nepal.

Close by the Kâlî shrine there is a hole in the verandah floor, where the sacred fire for the *hom* ceremony is lighted, and offerings given to Agni, the god of fire.

The temple, built about fifty years ago by the Raja of Ahmêty of Oudh, towering over Manikarnika ghât with its five deep-red spires and gilded pinnacles, is also dedicated to Durgâ. It is built on a terrace over-

MASK OF SHIVA

looking the river, and is approached by one of those steep, staircased streets, leading from the ghâts up into the city, which suggest a town of southern Italy or Spain. Clambering up a side staircase, you pass under the Naubat Khâna, where musicians are chanting praises of the goddess with strange but not unpleasing accompaniments. On the right side of the entrance is a fine little bronze lion of Durgâ, and on the left Shiva's bull. The quiet and cleanliness inside are a relief from the bustle, sloppiness, and dirt, and

IN THE AHMÊTY TEMPLE

A Brahmin performing his *sandhya*.

the somewhat sordid atmosphere of more popular Benares shrines. You will generally find here one or two Brahmins sitting devoutly at their *sandhya*, without pestering visitors for the eternal *bakshish*, and, unless there is some special festival, there is no great throng of pilgrims or other worshippers.

The temple itself is one of the most elegant in

THE AHMÊTY TEMPLE

Benares. Its cusped arches and graceful stone tracery betray the Saracenic influence, which is very prominent in modern Hindu art in northern India. The most interesting detail in the decoration is the row of winged figures under the main cornice, carved with all the naïveté and feeling of early Italian sculpture, though there is no reason to suppose that the Benares sculptors borrowed anything from European models. They represent the Gandharvas, the heavenly musicians, and the Apsarasas, the dancing girls of Indra's heaven—sirens who fascinated gods and lured holy men from their devotions.

The temple of Annapurna, the goddess of plenty, near the Golden Temple, is one of the most popular places of worship in Benares, and one of the few which Europeans are now allowed to enter. A number of beggars sit outside with bowls in front of them to collect rice and other donations from the passers-by. One of them, who is maintained by the Brahmin proprietors of the temple as a kind of living advertisement, is a most uncanny object. Enormously fat, stark naked except for a small loin-cloth, his head shaved, and his whole brown body smeared with a thick layer of Ganges mud, he looks, as he squats on the ground and gazes up with curious hazel eyes under his puffed-up eyelids, more like some huge batrachian than anything human. He is given enough food to gorge himself daily, and passes his life in this state of semi-torpor at the temple entrance. Through hot weather and cold weather he has sat at the same spot, day after day, as long as the oldest inhabitant can remember, fed by Annapurna, so they say, for the last hundred years.

The main entrance has two fine brass repoussé doors. Within the temple the stone steps and the floor of the courtyard are reeking with Ganges water, mixed with mud from the feet of the worshippers. The plan is very like that of the so-called Monkey Temple, but Annapurna is older and in better style, having been built about two hundred years ago. Cows, goats, and a constant throng of people fill the precincts. At one little corner near the side entrance Europeans are admitted, and here one can study the popular side of Hinduism at leisure. The usual ceremony observed by all who enter is, after presenting an offering of food or money to the Brahmin in attendance, to circumambulate the shrine a number of times, keeping the right hand towards it, and pausing in front of it to salute the image of the goddess. Some touch the sill of the temple porch with their foreheads; others rub their fingers in the mud, and touch their foreheads and their eyes with it. "To the pure all things are pure"—and Annapurna is so pure, they believe, that even the dirt in her temple is purity. A Brahmin sits at one corner to place a red mark on the centre of each worshipper's forehead. Before leaving, many will go up into the porch and strike a bell which hangs in the centre.

Some of the women, especially Brahmin widows, who can be distinguished by the sacred texts printed all over their *saris*, sprinkle Ganges water in spoonfuls from their lotas, and scatter rice and flowers on the idols placed in the verandahs round the quadrangle —Hanuman, Ganêsha, and Surya.

A gaunt and wild-looking old man, nearly naked and tottering with fatigue, crawls into the temple quadrangle and round it many times, stretching himself full-length on the sloppy floor at every step, and only pausing to salute the goddess as he passes in front of the shrine. He has just come from making the pilgrimage of the Panch-kôsi road—fifty weary miles in the same way—in fulfilment of a vow.

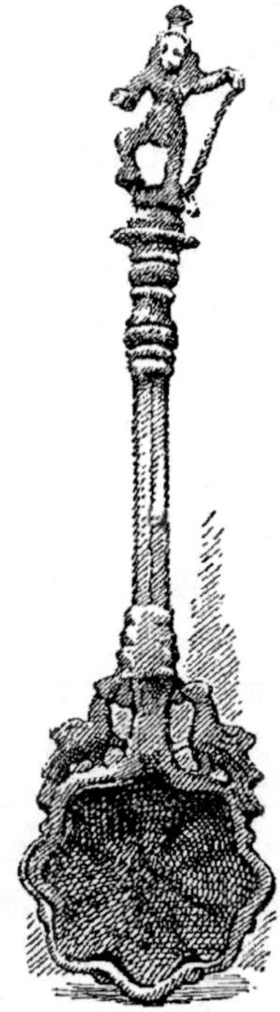

A SACRIFICIAL SPOON

Many are the objects for which Hindus will perform such penances, sometimes to acquire worldly advantages in the present life—for they believe that the merit they acquire will sooner or later be rewarded in some tangible form—sometimes to excite pity and to collect alms, perhaps for religious purposes, or perhaps for a dowry for a daughter—sometimes in hopes of vengeance on an enemy, to be gratified in a future incarnation.

Another man spends half an hour with intense seriousness before the monkey god, Hanuman, rubbing the limbs of the image with the most tender solicitude, as if the massage would be pleasing to the deity, and muttering prayers and formulas continually. On the floor of the porch, in front of the shrine, quantities of sweetmeats, rice, and other grain are collected—charitable offerings for Annapurna to distribute; for, in a land where famine afflicts the people so sorely, Annapurna's aid is often wanted. Many poor mothers bring their children to be fed in the upper gallery which runs round the quadrangle. Birds and animals share in Annapurna's bounty, and, as everywhere in Benares, help to make delightful pictures. Pigeons fly down and peck up the grains of rice from Ganêsha's grotesque body, goats and cattle munch the wreaths of marigolds which, on festival days, are piled in golden heaps about the quadrangle. Two Bengali youths stop to kiss and caress a cow, as it basks contentedly in a sunny corner, after its meal of marigolds. It responds to their endearments with signs of intense enjoyment more usual in a dog than in the stolid bovine nature.

A few links of an iron chain, smooth and polished by frequent handling, hang on a door-post at the side entrance. Many of the worshippers as they pass out take hold of them, and touch first the left eye, then the right, and then the two sides of the chest, for iron is believed to be a charm against the evil influence of Saturn, the most unlucky of all the planets. Poor souls! perhaps the evil-eyed one has grievously afflicted them. The shrine of Sanîchar, as he is called, is not far from Annapurna. Seven and a half years is said to be the time during which he troubles the unhappy ones who come under his influence.

From the Hindu stand-point, the most holy and interesting of all the Benares temples is that which is dedicated to Vishweshwar, or Shiva as the patron deity of Benares. It is situated in the same narrow street as Annapurna, and is even more crowded with worshippers than the temple of the goddess of plenty. Europeans are not allowed to enter, but they can look down upon it from a balcony just opposite—the Naubat Khana or "music house", where the big temple drums are kept. It is called the Golden Temple, from the fact of its dome and spires being covered with gilt repoussé copper work, a gift of Ranjit Singh of Lahore. There is nothing particularly noticeable in this modern Sikh decoration, nor is there anything else in the temple artistically or architecturally attractive.

THE TEMPLE AT RAMNAGAR

(By permission of H. H. the Maharaja of Benares.)

The same may be said of nearly all the rest of the hundreds of small modern temples with which the city is crowded. Many of them are described by Sherring, in his *Sacred City of the Hindus*, with great minuteness, but without much sense of artistic proportion. In design and sculptured decoration the temple of Durgâ, at Ramnagar, on the side of the river opposite to Benares, is a very good example of modern Indian temple architecture. It was commenced by Raja Chêt Singh in the last half of the eighteenth century, and finished about 1850. Chêt Singh also constructed a fine bathing tank at Ramnagar, which is frequented by large crowds in the month of Magh (January–February). Vedavyâs, the reputed compiler of the Vedas, is said to have appointed Ramnagar to be a place of pilgrimage in that month, so that those who performed it might be relieved of the penalty of being re-incarnated as asses, which they would otherwise incur if they happened to die on this side of the river.

The palace of the Maharaja of Benares, an imposing pile of buildings on the river bank, is also at Ramnagar. It contains a fine library, including a splendidly illustrated copy of the Râmâyana, and a very interesting collection of old Indian paintings.

Some of the Benares temples, though architecturally unimportant, are interesting as illustrating the ideas of Hindu mythology and popular superstitions. One at Manikarnika, next to the women's bathing ghât, named Tarâkeshwar, is so called from the belief that to worshippers at this shrine Shiva will whisper in their ear while dying a *mantram*, called Tarâk, which will secure admission into his paradise. Another called Barahan Devi, near Man-Mandil ghât, is resorted to by those who have swellings in the hands or feet. The temple of Briddhkâl is supposed to have been granted by Shiva the virtue of curing all kinds of diseases, and of prolonging life. Sukreswar, near the Golden Temple, is believed to bestow beautiful sons on those who worship at the shrine.

Bhaironath, whose chief temple is not far from the town-hall, is the *kotwal*, or spiritual magistrate of

Benares. He exercises jurisdiction over the whole of the district within the limits of the Panch-kôsi road, and is supposed to act as defender of the Hindu faith and to keep away evil spirits. His *vahan*, or vehicle, is a dog; for this reason dogs, which are excluded from other temples, are admitted into his.

MASK OF BHAIRONATH

His weapon is a huge club, which receives worship as well as his own image. The officiating priest is armed with a rod of peacock's feathers, with which he punishes the worshippers for the offences they have committed, and at the same time absolves them. There are very interesting copper or silver masks of Bhaironath sometimes to be found in Benares. An unfinished, but very expressive one, suggestive of an Egyptian mummy, is here illustrated.

Ganêsha, the son of Shiva, has many temples in the city. Being the god of wisdom, he is the especial patron of school-boys and authors. He is invoked by merchants before all business transactions. He is also the keeper of roads and the protector of households. In the latter capacity his vehicle is a rat—an association of ideas which would not commend itself to modern plague specialists. There are several popular legends to account for this deity and his extravagant appearance. One is that, while Shiva was away from home, Parvati, his wife, took a bath, and to guard her apartments from intruders, fashioned Ganêsha from the scurf of her body and placed him at the door. Shiva, returning, was angry at being opposed by the unknown doorkeeper, and cut off Ganêsha's head. Parvati was indignant at her husband's violence, and refused to be pacified. Shiva then gave orders to his attendants to search for a living creature that slept with its head towards the north, to cut off its head, and to fit it upon Ganêsha's body. The first creature they found was an elephant. So Ganêsha goes to this day with an elephant's head. The same story is given as an explanation why Hindus should not sleep with the head towards the north.

This sad misadventure apparently did not teach caution to the god of wisdom, for on a subsequent occasion he lost a tusk in trying to oppose the entrance of another visitor, Parashu-Râma, one of the incarnations of Vishnu, into Shiva's abode. He is known on this account as Eka-danta, "the one-tusked".

The Hindu pilgrim holds in high veneration the sacred wells of Benares, but until recently their in-

GANÊSHA

conceivable foulness, caused by the decay of floral offerings constantly thrown into them, rendered them anything but attractive to Europeans. In the last few years a great deal has been done for the sanitation of Benares, both by the municipality and by the exertions of a private society founded in honour of Queen Victoria's jubilee, so that most of the wells are now approachable. Few of them, however, are artistically interesting, except the Gyân-kûp. The famous well at Manikarnika, the starting-point of every pilgrim's round of ceremonies, has been already described. The Gyân-kûp, or well of knowledge, stands in the large quadrangle between the Golden Temple and the mosque of Aurangzîb, which is built on the site of the old Vishweshwar temple. It is covered by a graceful Saracenic colonnade, erected in 1828 by the widow of Doulat Rao Scindhia of Gwalior. The colossal stone bull of Shiva, close by, is a very picturesque accessory, and the crowds of pilgrims always give much to observe and study. A Brahmin sits by the well with a ladle to give each pilgrim a sip of the water. The colonnade is a favourite resting-place, and there you may often see pilgrims, who carry with them the image and symbols of their patron deity, arranging a little shrine on the floor and going through all the prescribed forms of *pûjâ*.

The legend connected with this well is that once upon a time Benares was suffering from a great drought. No rain had fallen for twelve years, and the city was in a terrible plight. At last a Rishi, one of the great Hindu sages, or divinely-inspired prophets, grasping the trident of Shiva, thrust it into the earth at this spot. A spring of water immediately bubbled up, sufficient to relieve the misery of the whole city. Shiva, on hearing of the miracle, took up his abode in the well, and remains there to this day. Another legend, perhaps with more historical foundation, says that when the old temple of Vishweshwar was destroyed by Aurangzîb, a priest took the idol and threw it down the well.

THE WELL OF KNOWLEDGE

Not far from the temple of Bhaironath is the Well of Fate—Kâl-kûp—in which a square hole is arranged over the trellis-work surrounding the well, so that at noon the sun's rays strike on the water below. He who looks down in the well at this hour and cannot see his own shadow in the water is a doomed man, for he will surely die within six months, unless he can persuade Mahâ-kâl, "Great Fate", or Shiva, whose temple adjoins the well, to intervene with Yama, the god of death, on his behalf. The clocks of Benares are set by Madras time, which is some minutes behind the true local time, so the well is likely to be a source of much anxiety to ignorant pilgrims, and corresponding profit to the proprietors of the temple.

Another interesting well is the Nâg-kûân, in which a great snake is said to reside. Indian folk-lore is full of legends of the snake-king and the snake-people—powerful sorcerers who could assume human shape at will—who lived below the water in palaces glittering with gold and jewels. The Nâg-râja who lives in this well is propitiated by offerings of milk. Once a year, in the month of Sawan, a pilgrimage is made to the well, and Nâg-pûjâ, or worship of the snake-god, is performed by crowds of pilgrims. The well is approached by four flights of steep stone steps. In a niche placed in the wall over one of the sides is a shrine of the snake-god. The steps leading to the well were constructed or put in order about 150 years ago, but the well itself is doubtless of great antiquity.

CHAPTER X

THE PANCH-TIRTH AND THE PILGRIMAGE OF THE PANCH-KÔSI ROAD—THE PILGRIMAGE OF THE SOUL

One of the spiritual aids which Benares is supposed to afford to Hindus is that it contains within its limits various shrines constituted by Brahminical authority as equal in sanctity to the most sacred places of Hindu pilgrimage, such as Allahabad, where the Jumna joins the Ganges; Kedarnath, in the Himalayas; or Rameswaram, in the extreme south. The pilgrim, therefore, without the toilsome journeys which the longer distances involve, can obtain all the merit and spiritual benefit he desires by visiting certain shrines in Benares, specially distinguished from the thousands it contains.

One of the pilgrimages is known as the Panch-tirth, from the five holy places the pilgrim must visit, namely, Asi Sangam, where the river Asi joins the Ganges, Dasâsamedh Ghât, the well at Manikarnika, Panchganga Ghât, and Barna Sangam, at the extreme north. He will thus have traversed the whole length of the ghâts from the south to the north.

But the most interesting and the most meritorious of all the pilgrimages is that of the Panch-kôsi road, the sacred road which limits the area of Benares on the land side. Throughout its length of about fifty miles, it is reckoned to be at a distance of panch-kôs, or five kôs,[1] from Manikarnika well. It is believed by the Hindus to be of great antiquity, and I see no reason to doubt this, though Sherring discredits the tradition. It is possible that the alignment of the road may have varied from time to time, but the practice of circumambulating a shrine, or other holy place, is one of the most ancient of religious observances, and it is interesting to note that the recent Tibet expedition found crowds of Buddhist pilgrims circumambulating the sacred city of Lhasa.

The pilgrimage of the Panch-kôsi road is now one which every Hindu inhabitant of Benares is enjoined to make, especially every third year, in the intercalary month which regulates the Hindu lunar calendar. The merit ascribed to this pilgrimage is immense. All the sins which have been committed within the limits of the city can be expiated by the proper fulfilment of the rules of the journey, for along this road the pilgrims circumambulate all that is holy in the holiest of cities. Manikarnika is the starting-point. They must walk on foot without shoes, except in the case of the sick or infirm, taking with them only necessary food, without luxuries of any kind. They must refrain from quarrelling or using bad language. They must not give or receive food or water, nor take any gift from anyone. But as human nature is the same all the world over, the wealthier pilgrims often find means to soften the austerities of the journey by arranging with members of their own family, who are not making the pilgrimage, to meet them at the different halting-places with food and other comforts.

Whatever we may think of the special virtues attri-

[1] A kôs is about two miles.

buted by Hindus to the pilgrimage, there is no doubt that there is a great charm about this old country road in the crisp air of a late December morning, and something of the Vedic spirit in the simple piety of the old traditions which cling to it. From Manikarnika the crowd of pilgrims, young and old, rich and poor, wend their way along the ghâts to Asi. Sangam on the south, where the little stream called Asi flows into the Ganges. Crossing this, a path leads along the river for some distance through fields of wheat and barley, then widens out into a broad avenue lined by splendid mango-trees. Framed in the noble colonnade of their massive trunks and the deep rich foliage are vistas of tender green cornfields, varied with clumps of sugar-cane, patches of yellow mustard and marigold, and the lilac of linseed flowers. The pilgrims pause to pay their devotions at the little wayside shrines placed between the trees. At one place the road is strewn for some distance with broken moulds, where a colony of brass-workers is engaged in making the vessels for which Benares is famous. Next we pass a Hindu monastery.

The first day's halting-place is at Khandawa, a typical Hindu village, six miles from Manikarnika along the sacred road. As you approach it you may see a kid lying by the roadside, sacrificed by some low-caste villagers to appease the spirits of evil. Here a bamboo with a red flag marks the altar of Dêvi, perhaps the Earth goddess of the Dasyus, or another of the primitive aboriginal divinities afterwards brought into the Hindu pantheon as one of the wives of Shiva. At a little distance from the village is the usual collection of huts occupied by potters, rope and basket

THE PANCH-KÔSI ROAD

makers, and others whose low-caste occupations render them undesirable as inhabitants. These locations are survivals of the early Aryan times when the dark-skinned Dasyu slaves, who plied the lowest trades, were not allowed within the Aryan pale. The potters are twirling the clay on the primitive native wheel a relic of almost prehistoric times, and women with a stately pose and gait are carrying on their heads the finished vessels, baked in a heap of cow-dung fuel, for sale in the village.

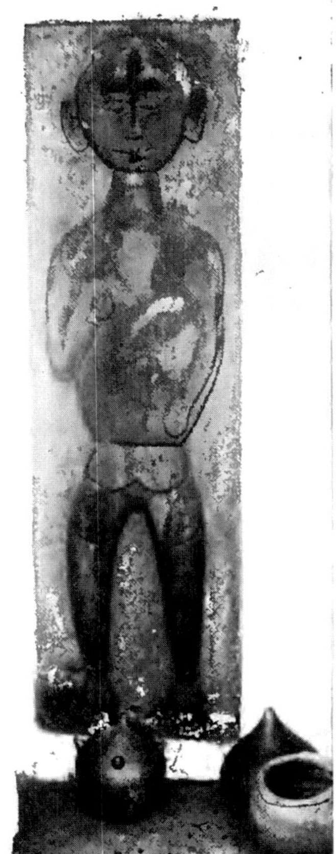

A VILLAGE DEITY

Another roadside shrine farther on contains a rude carving of an ancient village deity, hardly higher in the artistic scale than the fetish of a South Sea savage. Beyond this a row of magnificent tamarind trees, whose gnarled and twisted trunks prove their venerable age, affords a grateful shade for the pilgrims, and a splendid portico for one of the *dharmsalas*, or rest-houses, in which they may halt and take their food. The village itself is nestled round a spacious tank, one of those splendid public works which Hindu rulers and pious benefactors of olden days bestowed on their posterity.

It is a refreshing contrast to the narrow, crowded streets of the city, the dirt, bustle and unrest, the plethora of monstrous idols and their never-ending rites—this broad expanse of placid water mirroring the tall red spire of a fine old temple, and the dense, rich foliage of the sacred trees which cluster round it. It is in the village life, and not in the life of the crowded cities, that Hinduism is seen at its best. The organization of the village communities, dating back from the

THE TEMPLE AND TANK AT KHANDAWA

earliest Aryan settlements, has still in some parts of India survived all the storms of contending races and creeds, and remained the political unit of the state. The change which British administration has brought about in this respect seems to be a doubtful advantage. The ordinary affairs of such village communities are administered by a hereditary headman, or *patel*, assisted by a council of elders called the *panchayet*, exercising certain kinds of judicial and legislative powers, and acting as intermediaries between the government and the people. Among the recognized officials, having specific duties and privileges, are hereditary police, traders, and artisans; the priest who performs religious ceremonies, and sometimes the dancing girl who assists at festivities; the *guru* who is the village schoolmaster, and the accountant who acts as finance minister for these miniature republics. They are paid by allowances of grain, or by the grant of cultivated land as hereditary possessions.

Khandawa, however, has not retained its ancient Hindu constitution, but has become part of a zemindary, the system of private proprietorship which grew out of the Mogul method of collecting land-revenue. The old temple is one of the few within the limits of Benares which date farther back than the first Muhammadan invasion. It is much bolder and finer in style than the modern Benares temples. Embedded in one side of the portico are a few fragments of sculpture belonging to a still older shrine. Among them is a piece of vigorous carving of those quaint and playful dwarf-like figures which are frequent in Indian sculpture of the early Buddhist times, when the disembodied spirit was believed to resemble a human dwarf in size and appearance. The only touch of modernity about the temple is an English eight-day clock, presented by the owner of the village, so that its inhabitants might know the time of day. It is hung up inside the shrine over the phallic emblem of Shiva.

Round about the temple are picturesquely grouped

ANCIENT CARVING, KHANDAWA TEMPLE

several smaller shrines. They each contain a few pieces of old sculpture, representing one or other of the 300,000,000 deities the Hindu pantheon is said to contain. The Hindu peasant is as confirmed an idolater as the Muhammadan is iconoclast. With a profound indifference to archæological or sectarian distinctions he will take a fragment of sculpture, Buddhist, Jain, or Hindu, headless, armless, or legless, build a little shrine for it, give it the name which pleases him best, and worship it as a manifestation of his favourite divinity.

Along the four sides of the tank are broad avenues of trees. Under them the cattle tread out the corn and turn the slow, creaking mill which crushes the juicy sugar-cane. Their mangers, like village altars, are raised on mud pedestals between the trees. Beyond the neat thatched huts an endless expanse of ripening crops promises a plenteous harvest.

Leaving Khandawa, the pilgrims continue their journey by the shady road through the fertile fields, and on the second day reach Dhupchandi, a village eight miles farther on. The third day's journey of fourteen miles brings them to Râmeswar, and to a temple there dedicated to Râma. On the fourth they arrive at Shivapur, eight miles farther. Here there is a tank and a Shiva temple containing a number of shrines in which fragments of ancient sculpture are set up for worship, including one of the Panch Pândavas, the five heroes of the Mahâbhârata, and one of Surya, the sun-god, in his seven-horsed car.

At Kapildhara, the fifth day's stage, six miles beyond Shivapur, the pilgrims offer oblations to the Pitris, the souls of the ancestors. It is one of the places deemed propitious for the *Shradha* ceremonies of deceased relatives, which are believed to help the souls of the departed on their final pilgrimage to Yama-puri, the kingdom of Death.

According to the Hindu doctrine of the future life, there are two paths, followed by souls of different states of development, according to their karma. The saints who have fulfilled their karma travel by the Devayana, the way of the gods, through the rays of the sun, and never return to be reborn on earth.

Ordinary souls, which have yet to finish the cycle of transmigrations, travel by the Dhumayana of the seven planes, but they can only reach two—Swar-loka, heaven, or Bhuvar-loka, the astral plane, according to the life they have led in the world. The souls of ordinary mortals will, it is believed, always remain tied to earth, and eventually become evil spirits tormenting mankind, unless the *Shradha* ceremonies are duly performed to help them on their way to Yama.

For the first ten days after death the ceremonies performed by the relatives are to help the disembodied

"Thin vaporous clouds of smoke rise from the funeral pyres. The slanting rays of the morning sun cast long shadows across the ghat" (page 137)

spirit to obtain a form, or prêta-body, which will carry it on its appointed pilgrimage. This is supposed to be effected by the *pinda* offerings, the food presented to the spirit (consisting of barley or rice-flour, mixed with sesamum flour, sugar, and honey), and by the recitation of appropriate *mantras*. The first day's ceremony furnishes the spirit with a head, the next a neck and shoulders. When the prêta-body is fully formed, on the tenth day, it feeds on the pinda and offerings of milk.

On the thirteenth day after death, the soul is equipped for its solemn journey. There are twelve stages in the pilgrimage, each stage taking a month to accomplish. Throughout the twelve months the relatives follow the departed spirit with the *Shradha* ceremonies, sixteen in number, performed at stated times to provide it with sustenance and to prepare it for the goal.

When that at last is reached, the prêta-body is dissolved. The soul now becomes a Pitri, and assumes another body adapted for enjoying heavenly bliss, or for suffering the pains of hell. In this state it appears before the judge, Yama, the Lord of Pitris.

To those who have lived virtuous lives, Yama has a pleasant and glorious aspect when he receives the pilgrims into the bliss of Swarga. He has four arms, bearing a conch-shell, a discus, a mace, and a lotus. He rides, like Vishnu, on a mighty eagle, Garuda. A splendid crown adorns his brow, and jewelled ornaments glitter in his ears. His complexion is like the blue lotus, a gracious smile beams on his lips. He wears a sacred thread like gold on his breast, and a garland of forest flowers on his neck.

But to the sinners Yama appears in a gigantic and terrific shape, with black complexion and eyes vast as lakes. His nostrils breathe fire. His bristling hairs stand out long and thick like rushes. His deep voice sounds like the thunder of the Last Day. He is mounted on a ferocious buffalo, and holds a mighty club in his hand.

When the souls have enjoyed their bliss, or suffered their allotted punishment, they are again re-incarnated on earth to fulfil the remainder of their karma.

This belief in the efficacy of *Shradhas* is often the source of reckless expenditure bringing ruin upon Hindu families. For not only do the dead require assistance in their pilgrimage to Yama's kingdom, but for three generations afterwards they are supposed to need the attention of their descendants. Moreover, the mantras and ceremonies performed at certain holy places are believed to have the power of mitigating the penalties for sins committed in this life, an idea sedulously fostered by the Brahmin priests, though it is absolutely inconsistent with their own teaching of the law of karma.

With this digression we will return to the Panchkôsi road. The sixth and last stage of the pilgrimage is from Kapildhara to Barna Sangam, and thence along the ghâts to the starting-place, Manikarnika. On this day the pilgrims carry bags of barley, from which they scatter grain all along the route, as an oblation to Shiva. Arriving at Manikarnika, they bathe in the river and give presents to the Brahmins. Finally they proceed to the temple of Sâkhi-Vinayak, the witness-bearing Ganêsha, to have the fact of the pilgrimage attested by the priest, in presence of the deity.

CHAPTER XI

REMAINS OF OLD BENARES—A HINDU-MUHAMMADAN RIOT—A WEAVERS' COLONY

A thorough examination by trained archæologists of the ruins and fragments of sculpture which are scattered about Benares and built into modern shrines and temples might throw much light on the ancient history of the city. Hitherto this work has been left chiefly to Europeans without sufficient critical knowledge of Hindu art, whose judgment has been biassed by a fixed idea that nearly everything old in Benares is of Buddhist origin. Sherring, while recognizing the probability of many of the antiquities of the city being of Brahminical or Jain origin, is too much inclined to attribute to Buddhists every ancient column with a plain bracket capital and every stone carved with the lotus flower.

Fergusson's review of Indian architectural styles, admirable though it is, stands in need of explanation and modification in the light of recent knowledge. In his time it was hardly realized that Buddhism was only an offshoot of Hinduism, which grew up in India, flourished, and decayed side by side with dozens of other sects of even older origin, some of which, like the Jains, were most active builders.

The artistic study of Indian sculpture, like that of

Indian painting, has hardly yet been commenced, though there is much of extreme interest to the artist, as well as to the archæologist, in both. It is very unlikely that rapid progress will be made in this direction until Indians of education and means learn the profound truth of Emerson's well-known aphorism, "Art is Nature passed through the alembic of man"; and until they begin to realize that, unless they understand and appreciate the value of the presentment of Nature their own artist-alchemists have given them, nothing that they see through European spectacles has any artistic value or meaning for them.

In the meantime, while Indian art is fast decaying beyond all hope, it is left to a few Europeans to attempt the solution of problems which to competent Indians should be comparatively easy.

Scattered about Benares in odd corners, and placed under pippal and banian trees for worship, are numbers of miniature temples elaborately carved in single blocks of stone, and all of them with the characteristic Hindu *sikra* or curvilinear spire. Some of them are multiple shrines, that is, carved all over with numerous minute representations of temples, all of the same shape. The popular tradition about these is that Raja Mân Singh of Jaipur made a vow to present 100,000 temples to the city, and ordered them to be commenced and finished in one day. In order to accomplish this extraordinary architectural feat they were all carved in miniature.

The tale is obviously a Brahminical invention. These stones seem to be votive shrines of a very much earlier time than Mân Singh, who lived at the beginning of the seventeenth century. Many of them are of the early Buddhist period, and numbers of them are now being dug up in the neighbourhood of Sarnath. They are not, however, Buddhist, but dedicated to various Hindu deities. The Deer-park at Sarnath was, as we know, a retreat, or kind of sacred grove, where religious devotees of all sects met.

ANCIENT VOTIVE STONES

The most interesting of the ruined buildings of ancient Benares now existing are those which have been appropriated by the Muhammadans. At the back of the mosque of Aurangzîb, near the Golden Temple, is a fragment of what must have been a very imposing Brahminical or Jain temple. The south wall of the mosque is built into it. Tradition points to this as being part of the original temple of Vishweshwar destroyed by Aurangzîb. From the style it would appear to belong to the time of Akbar, or about the beginning of the sixteenth century. The raised terrace in front of the mosque is built upon some very much older structure, which Sherring suggests might have been a Buddhist vihâra or temple-monastery. This, however, is mere conjecture. On equally substantial grounds it might be supposed to be one of the public halls for the discussion of philosophical and religious subjects which existed in Buddhist and pre-Buddhist times. It is quite possible that the whole quadrangle in which the mosque stands originally contained a number of Brahminical, or perhaps Jain, temples and monasteries of many different periods, such as are often found grouped together in places considered especially sacred by any sect of Hindus. In the northern side of the city there are several Muhammadan mosques which have been built out of the remains of old Jain, Buddhist, or Brahminical temples or monasteries. The most interesting and picturesque of these is opposite to Kâsi railway-station. The Muhammadans, in converting it to their own use about one hundred and twenty years ago, gave it a symmetry suggestive of a Greek or Roman temple.

There are several other mosques of the same kind in the same part of the city. The Arhâî Kangûra mosque is a large one in the quarter bearing that name, constructed in the same way from abandoned or demolished Hindu or Buddhist buildings. In the roof of the second story a slab is inserted, upon which is a long Sanskrit inscription, and the date 1191 A.D., showing that it originally belonged to a Hindu temple or monastery. The Muhammadans, iconoclasts as they were, have been more respectful to ancient art in Benares than British utilitarians like the district officer mentioned by General Cunningham,[1] who carted away a quantity of statues and carved stones excavated from Sarnath to strengthen the foundations of the bridge over the Barna.

Within the area of the old Raj Ghât Fort, and not far from Kâsi station, is one of the few original Mu-

TOMB OF LÂL KHAN

hammadan buildings in Benares which are specially noteworthy for architectural beauty. This is a fine monument, as rich in colour as cloisonné enamel, the whole surface of the exterior and interior being decorated with tiles, in the style which the Muhammadans introduced into India from Persia and Central Asia. It is the tomb of Lâl Khan, a minister of a former Raja of Benares.

[1] Archæological Report, 1861–2, p. 123.

This form of decoration with coloured tiles and tile mosaic is closely related to the stone and marble mosaic and inlay which the Saracenic architects employed when they established themselves in countries where the latter materials were plentiful. The gradual change from tiles to marble mosaic and inlay can be easily traced in the Muhammadan buildings in Delhi and Agra, ending in the decoration of the Taj Mahal, which has been attributed to Italian designers on evidence which does not bear careful scrutiny.

The tomb at Raj Ghât was originally surrounded by a garden, but only the four corner towers of the enclosure now remain. The Moguls usually built their own tombs in gardens which were used as pleasure-grounds when their owners were alive, and consecrated to religion and the memory of the dead afterwards—an old Tartar custom which they brought with them into India. In the planting of the gardens they symbolized life with flowering trees and shrubs, and death and eternity with the evergreen cypress tree.

About a mile to the west of Raj Ghât, at the junction of the Ghazipur road with the Raj Ghât road, there are a large tank in a ruined state, called Kapilmochan Tank or Bhairo-ka Talao, and vestiges of ancient buildings of considerable extent, interesting to the archæologist, but not otherwise attractive. On a great terrace above the tank is the Lât Bhairo, already alluded to, which is believed to be the fragment of one of the columns put up by Asoka to commemorate some event in the life of Buddha, or to record a proclamation of the faith. The Hindus in later times built a temple there dedicated to Bhairo, the god-magistrate of Benares. Aurangzîb destroyed the temple and built a mosque in its place. Since then the terrace has been a frequent battle-field for contending Hindu and Muhammadan factions.

The Hindus, after the destruction of their temple, continued to worship the lât, which was then about 40 feet high, as an emblem of Shiva. They were permitted to do so by the Muhammadans on condition that the custodians of the mosque received a share of the offerings. About the beginning of the last century the jealousy between the rival religionists led to an outbreak in which the lât was thrown down and broken to pieces. The circumstances which caused the disturbance are such a fruitful source of serious riots even in the present day that the details given by a contemporary writer[1] may be interesting. It so happened that at the Mohurram, the great Muhammadan festival, and the Holi, a somewhat licentious celebration very popular with the lower classes of Hindus, the processions of both parties, inflamed with religious excitement, *bhang*, and alcohol, met in the streets, and, as usual on such occasions, neither party would yield a passage. A free fight followed, and the Muhammadans were beaten. In revenge some of them rushed to the courtyard of Aurangzîb's mosque and overthrew the sacred lât of Bhairo, while others seized a sacred cow and killed it on the ghâts, mingling its blood with the water of the Ganges.

Now there was a tradition that the lât had been originally much higher. It was said that it had been gradually sinking, and that, when the top became level with the ground, all nations would become of one caste, or, in other words, all Hindus would be out-

[1] Rev. William Buyers in *Recollections of Northern India.*

casted. The overthrow of the lât was interpreted as a fulfilment of the prophecy, and the outrage on their deepest religious sentiments roused the whole of the Hindu population to fury. Headed by the Brahmin priests, the sannyâsin, and all the religious devotees of Benares, a furious mob seized any sort of weapon within reach. A general massacre of the Muhammadans and the destruction of every mosque in the city was only prevented by the intervention of the British authorities. At this crisis the native Sepoys behaved splendidly. Many of them were Brahmins, whose sympathies were entirely with their co-religionists; but, nevertheless, when posted to guard the mosques, they never wavered for a moment in loyalty to their officers, but kept off the infuriated mob at the point of the bayonet.

Order was at last restored, but the excitement remained for many days afterwards. The double sacrilege was regarded by the Brahmins as a stain which might have destroyed the sanctity of the city as a place of Hindu pilgrimage. The scene which followed is thus described by Mr. Buyers: "All the Brahmins of the city, many thousands in number, went down in deep sorrow to the river-side, naked and fasting, and sat on the principal ghâts, with folded hands and heads hanging down, to all appearance inconsolable, and refusing to enter a house or to taste food".

After two or three days' fast, however, they, yielding to the persuasion of the magistrates, and others who went to comfort them, decided that Ganges' purity was inviolable, and that the desecration of the city could be purged by a series of costly ceremonies.

The chief English official who brought the unhappy

An idyll of peace and self-satisfaction" (page 155)

event to a satisfactory termination was much impressed by the evident distress of the people. "The gaunt, squalid figures of the devotees, their visible and apparently unaffected anguish and dismay, the screams and outcries of the women, and the great numbers thus assembled, altogether constituted a spectacle of woe such as few cities but Benares could supply."

The famous lât of Bhairo is now reduced to a height of a few feet. It is covered with copper sheeting, painted red, and worshipped as a lingam. No Muhammadan is permitted to approach it.

At Bakariya Kund, in the northern quarter, there are also remains of ancient buildings, adapted by the Muhammadans, and a ruined tank. Except to ardent archæologists, there is more human interest in the colony of weavers close by, making the cloth of gold and silver, the rich brocaded silks and muslins for which Benares is famous.

The preparation of the silk for the looms is made in the open air, under the trees. Very beautiful it is to see the long lines of crimson, saffron, or purple, vibrating with iridescent tints in the chequered light of sun and shade, and the men and women passing up and down twirling the spindles from which the gossamer-like thread is unwound.

Watching this, one realizes the favourite simile of the Vedic poets, likening their hymns to the weaver's web stretched between earth and heaven; the priests and the people weaving into it the weft of sacrifice and prayers unceasingly, until the glorious fabric of immortality was made.

CHAPTER XII

BENARES UNDER BRITISH RULE

Benares for a brief period played a very conspicuous part in the early history of the British empire, and filled an eventful chapter in the life of the first governor-general. The treatment of Raja Chêt Singh of Benares by Warren Hastings was one of the principal indictments against the latter in the famous seven years' trial.

Under Mogul rule Benares ceased to have any great political importance, and when that empire crumbled to pieces after the death of Aurangzîb, the city and district became subject to the Nawab of Oudh. In 1775 Warren Hastings, who had previously interfered to prevent the Nawab from confiscating the zemindary, concluded a treaty by which the feudatory rights of Oudh were transferred to the British Government. The latter then granted a charter to Raja Chêt Singh confirming him in his possessions, subject to an annual fixed rent or tribute, and conferring upon him various rights and privileges which he had not enjoyed before. These concessions nevertheless did not prevent the Raja from taking advantage of the extraordinary difficulties of Warren Hastings' position to evade his obligations as a vassal and dependent of the East India Company.

The financial embarrassments of the Company, increased by the terrible famine of 1770, the wars with Haidar Ali in Mysore and with the Mahrattas in Bombay, had forced Hastings to call upon the Raja for further monetary aid and a special contingent of troops. The right of the sovereign power to exact such aid from its vassals was indisputable. Under the Mogul rule any disobedience to such demands would have been visited with confiscation of the vassal's possessions, and imprisonment, or death. But Chêt Singh, who was well informed of the dissensions in the Council at Calcutta, and of the critical state of the Company's affairs, hoped that with diplomatic procrastination he might soon be in a position to defy the British power. He paid the first year's subsidy with an ill grace and protestations of poverty, the next year's not until two battalions of Sepoys had been quartered upon him, and the Company's troops in the field had been reduced to dire distress for want of money. The demand for a contingent of cavalry was not complied with at all.

In 1781 Hastings felt himself strong enough to bring the recalcitrant Raja to account. Francis, his bitterest enemy, had retired to England after the historic duel, to vent his malice with fresh schemes and misrepresentations. The difficulties with Impey and the Supreme Court, brought about by the foolish attempt to impose the strict letter of the English law upon Indian courts of justice, had been arranged satisfactorily. On the other hand, the straits to which the Company's finances had been reduced made it imperative to raise fresh funds without further delay.

On the 7th July Hastings left Calcutta by river.

At Buxar, near to the boundary of the Benares zemindary, Chêt Singh met him with a fleet of boats crowded with two thousand well-armed troops. This, as Hastings observes in his narrative, was a deviation from the rules of decorum between vassals and their superiors, for the Governor-General had taken with him only a very small escort.

The Raja, however, had not yet the courage to show open hostility, but, placing his turban in Hastings' lap, tried to keep up an appearance of humility, with many vows and protestations of sincerity. Hastings received him civilly, but telling him plainly of his displeasure and determination to enforce the demands of Government, closed the interview. He arrived at Benares on the morning of the 14th of August. The Raja came a few hours later, but was forbidden to come to the Governor-General's quarters at Madhu Das's gardens, and ordered to await a communication from the Resident. The next morning Hastings sent the latter with a letter formulating charges of disaffection and infidelity to the Government, based on the Raja's previous conduct, with a demand for an immediate answer. Chêt Singh replied in terms which Hastings characterized as "not only unsatisfactory in substance, but offensive in style, and less a vindication of himself than a recrimination on me".

The Resident then received orders to repair next morning with his guard to the Raja's palace at Shivâla Ghât, to place Chêt Singh under arrest and to await further orders. The latter submitted quietly, but by some fatal mistake, or carelessness, the two companies of Sepoys who were placed in charge of the palace had taken no ammunition with them. The excitement among Chêt Singh's followers was intense, and before any steps could be taken to repair the blunder, large bodies of armed men crossed the river from the Raja's Fort at Ramnagar, surrounded the palace, and fell upon the sepoy guard. The reinforcements which were sent arrived too late to prevent the massacre which followed.

During the tumult Chêt Singh escaped to Ramnagar by lowering himself from one of the windows of the palace, for the river was in high flood and boats could be brought close under the palace walls.

The position of Hastings was then critical in the extreme. "If Chêt Singh's people," as he observes, "after they had effected his rescue, had proceeded to my quarters at Mahadew Das's Garden, instead of crowding after him in a tumultuous manner, as they did in his passage over the river, it is most probable that my blood, and that of about thirty English gentlemen of my party, would have been added to the recent carnage, for they were over two thousand in number, furious and daring from the easy success of the last attempt, nor could I assemble more than fifty regular and armed Sepoys for my whole defence."

Warren Hastings does not overestimate the dangers of the situation to the whole British empire in India when he adds: "Such a stroke as that which I have supposed would have been universally considered as decisive of the national fate; every state around it would have started into arms against it, and every subject of its own dominion would according to their several abilities have become its enemy".

The history of British India is largely the history of the blunders of incompetent bureaucrats, and the struggles of capable men of action with an impossible official machinery. There is no doubt that the loss to the Government at that crisis of Hastings' administrative courage and genius would have been a blow from which the British power might never have recovered.

A fresh disaster added to the peril of the British community in Benares. Hastings, immediately on the news of the outbreak, had sent orders to Captain Mahaffre, commanding the remainder of the detachment near Mirzapur, to bring up his men without delay, but on no account to risk an attack on Ramnagar, which was strongly defended by the Raja's followers. That officer, profiting by what he believed to be an opportunity for distinguishing himself, in direct defiance of orders, attempted to rush the Fort, and paid the penalty with his own life and the loss of most of his men.

This success elated the enemy so much that they determined to assume the offensive and attack Hastings at his quarters in Madhu Das's Gardens. The whole British force there collected now amounted to only four hundred and fifty men, under Major Popham, and, finding his position indefensible, Hastings, with that officer's approval, determined to retreat to the fort of Chunar, a strong position higher up the river. The retreat of the little British force, accompanied by the whole British community of Benares, was effected in safety. Hastings then, in consultation with his most capable military adviser, prepared to collect reinforcements and to organize defensive and offensive war against the Raja.

In the meantime Chêt Singh, while still making feeble attempts to gain time by sending half-apologetic,

PANCHGANGA (page 150)
By permission of H.H. the Maharaja of Benares

half-defiant messages to Hastings at Chunar, had collected round him an army of over twenty thousand regular troops, and about the same number of irregulars. Half of Oudh was in insurrection, and some of the zemindars of Behar showed signs of disaffection. The general respect and loyalty which Hastings inspired here stood him in good stead. The Sepoys of his little garrison remained staunch, although their pay was four months in arrear. Immediately on news of his difficulties, the Nawab of Oudh sent supplies and troops, and came himself to Chunar to offer his services. The Nawab Saâdat Ali, in whose charge Hastings had been compelled to leave his wounded Sepoys at Benares, not only protected them from Chêt Singh's vengeance, but supplied them with provisions, money, and medical attendance.

It was not long before Hastings received sufficient reinforcements from the nearest British commanders to enable him to attack the enemy, and before the end of September Chêt Singh, whose incapacity and cowardice were only equalled by his duplicity, had been driven out of all his strongholds by Major Popham, and was a miserable refugee at Gwalior. On the 25th of that month, Hastings was back in his old quarters at Madhu Das's Gardens, and the whole country had returned to a state of tranquillity. Thus ended a formidable insurrection, crushed in a few weeks by Hastings' indomitable courage and resource. Chêt Singh being proved guilty, not only of open rebellion, but of the murder of defenceless travellers and prisoners of war, was formally deposed. The next lineal heir, Babu Mehipnarain, from whom the present Maharaja is descended, was then installed as Raja. The city of Benares was placed under a separate magistracy directly controlled by the Company.

Seventeen years after these events, Madhu Das's Gardens had another occupant — not the British Governor-General, but a deposed Indian prince. In 1797, Asaf-ud-daulah, Nawab of Oudh, died. His brother, Nawab Saâdat Ali, whose name we have heard before, was next in succession, failing legitimate male issue of the late sovereign. The throne, however, was claimed by Wazir Ali, a generous but headstrong and somewhat dissolute youth of seventeen, whom Asaf-ud-daulah had recognized as his son and heir, but whose legitimacy was disputed.

The British Government, represented by a weak and vacillating Governor-General, Sir John Shore, at first acknowledged his title and proclaimed him nawab, but a few months afterwards, persuaded by the representations of the opposite party, deposed him and brought the rival claimant, Saâdat Ali, to occupy the palace at Lucknow. Then, with a fatuity which deserved the consequences which ensued, Sir John placed Wazir Ali at Benares, a very hotbed of intrigue, close to the borders of Oudh, and gave him an allowance of £15,000 a year, wherewith to finance his schemes of vengeance upon the British Government.

From his retreat in Madhu Das's Gardens, Wazir Ali immediately commenced to plot against the British power with all the disaffected Muhammadan and Hindu nobles of northern India. He entered into correspondence with Zeman Shah, the Afghan ruler of Kandahar, who had invaded the Punjab with a large army, and was now threatening Delhi. His chief fellow-conspirators at Benares were Jagat Singh, a relation of the Raja, and Shionath, the leader of a gang of *Bankas*, licensed banditti, who could be hired for any adventure or scheme which promised plunder.

The Resident at Benares, and agent of the Governor-General, was then Mr. G. F. Cherry, an amiable sporting civilian of many accomplishments and social graces, but greatly wanting in political insight. Wazir Ali found it easy to conceal from him his treasonable designs, and neither the warnings of the judge, Mr. Samuel Davis, nor the representations of the military authorities and the police, sufficed to put the easy-going Resident on his guard.

Mr. Davis being in close touch with native society, was able to get reliable information of Wazir Ali's proceedings. Finding it impossible to arouse his chief to a sense of the impending danger, he reported the facts direct to the Calcutta Council. Fortunately for the British Empire, the Marquis Wellesley, who soon after the deposition of Wazir Ali had succeeded Sir John Shore as Governor-General, was a statesman of a very different stamp to his predecessor. Immediately he realized the situation he sent orders to Mr. Cherry to inform Wazir Ali that the Government had decided to remove him to Calcutta at once.

This was a terrible blow to the ex-nawab, whose plan was to seize a favourable opportunity, when the projected war with Tippu Sultan had depleted the British garrisons in northern India, to massacre all the Europeans in Benares, barricade the city, and wait for a general rising to prepare the way for the advance of Zeman Shah's army. At Calcutta, under the eyes of the British Government, he would be helpless, and all hopes of recovering his lost kingdom would be gone for ever.

Finding it impossible to persuade the Government to revoke these orders, Wazir Ali sent notice to Mr. Cherry that he would be ready to start on the 16th January, 1799, and would breakfast with him on the 14th. At the same time he warned his fellow-conspirators to prepare for immediate action. On the morning of the 14th, Wazir Ali and two hundred desperate followers, fully armed, each Muhammadan wrapped in a winding sheet dipped in Mecca's sacred well, started from Madhu Das's Gardens bent on the slaughter of every European in Benares.

On their way to the Resident's house they met Mr. Davis and his wife on an elephant returning from their usual morning ride. It was probably some superstitious idea such as forms the motive in many an Oriental's action, good or bad, which induced them to spare the very man who was destined to frustrate their evil designs, for after a hurried consultation they passed by with the usual salutation. Their first victim was a young civilian named Graham, who was on his way to breakfast with the magistrate. Him they dragged from his palanquin and killed on the spot.

When they reached the Residency, Mr. Cherry, still unsuspecting—in spite of repeated warnings from various quarters—received Wazir Ali with his usual friendliness, and took him in to breakfast. Four of the Nawab's escort, armed with swords, bucklers, and pistols, followed him to the table. As Mr. Cherry handed the first cup of tea to his principal guest, Wazir Ali began shouting in his face a fierce tirade against the Resident and the Government, ending with a defiant refusal to obey their orders. Then, as one of his followers moved to a chair at Mr. Cherry's side and pinioned his arms, Wazir Ali rose, seized the Resident by the collar, and slashed at him with his sword. The unfortunate man wrenched himself free, and rushed through the verandah into the garden, only to be cut to pieces by the ruffians outside. His private secretary, named Evans, who was also at the breakfast-table, and an officer staying in the house, were the next victims.

In the meantime Mr. Davis, who had received fresh warnings from the head of the police, had sent a messenger to Mr. Cherry, and was awaiting his return with anxiety. His worst fears were confirmed by the approach of Wazir Ali's murderous gang, and the sound of firing as they shot down the sentry posted at the entrance to his compound.

There was no time to be lost. He hurried his wife and two children, with their ayahs, up the narrow winding staircase which led to the only place of refuge—the terraced roof of the house, and rushed back for his firearms. It was too late! The ruffians were already at the door of the house. The only weapon within reach was a pike, over six feet long, used by one of his retainers. It was of iron, plated with silver, and had a sharp triangular steel blade. He seized this and retreated to the top of the staircase, prepared to defend single-handed the only approach to the roof on which his terror-stricken wife and children were crouching.

The mob hesitated for a moment. The stairs were narrow and steep, only admitting one at a time. An English sahib with a formidable pike was at the top. Then one more courageous than the rest crept up with drawn sword, while the others supported him from behind. A rapid thrust from the pike pierced his arm, and caused him to retire precipitately. Soon another ventured, and, more dexterous than the last, managed to evade the first thrust and to seize the pointed end of the pike. The brave magistrate replied to this manœuvre by dropping the shaft on the head of the staircase and, throwing his whole weight on it, jerked the point upwards. His assailant retired with his hands cut to the bone.

The howling mob turned heel also, after firing pistol volleys up the staircase, and commenced to smash the furniture, pillage the house and stables, and to murder any servants who interfered. An hour passed without any further attack—an hour of terrible suspense for Mr. Davis and the little party on the roof, who could only imagine the pandemonium downstairs by the crash of broken glass and furniture, and the shouting of Wazir Ali's myrmidons. The gallant defender of the staircase did not dare to move from his position, and one of the ayahs who ventured to peep over the parapet was shot through the arm.

Then the tumult suddenly ceased. Soon afterwards stealthy steps were heard upon the stairs, and, prepared for any cunning ruse of the enemy, Mr. Davis grasped his trusty spear and awaited the next attack. But this time it was the scared face of a faithful old servant, who held in front of him a rescued teapot as a sign of friendliness. He brought the welcome news of

Wazir Ali's retreat from the house. The arrival of fifteen armed policemen at the same time was a substantial reinforcement which relieved Mr. Davis from the intense strain of the situation.

The murder of the Resident had been the signal for all of Wazir Ali's adherents to rally round him and commence a general attack on the Europeans in the cantonment, some of whom concealed themselves in the fields of maize close by, while others fled to Bîtabûr, the military station ten miles from Benares, and gave the alarm. The general commanding, on the first intelligence, started off with his whole force. It was the approach of the British cavalry which drew off Wazir Ali's gang from the magistrate's house.

The rest of the story is soon told. Wazir Ali's men made a feeble attempt to harass the advanced guard, which arrived about eleven o'clock, but the infantry and guns, which followed soon afterwards, forced them to fall back on Madhu Das's Gardens. Here they made a last stand, but before the sun had set their resistance was broken, and the chief conspirators had fled to the hills. The only partakers in the miserable plot who played their part with any sort of distinction were Shionath and five of his gang of *Bankas*, who held at bay an overwhelming force of British troops for five hours, and then sallied out sword in hand to meet their fate like men.

Wazir Ali reached the Nepal Terai, and was joined by a few thousand adherents. A few defeats caused them to desert, and he was driven to take refuge at Jaipur. He was then extradited and brought as prisoner to Calcutta. After many years of close confinement in Fort William, he was sent to the State prison at Vellore, where he died.

Mr. Davis, whose clearness of judgment and personal courage probably averted a great disaster to the whole of British India, received only a formal letter of thanks from the Calcutta Council during the absence of the Marquis Wellesley at the seat of war in the south. He died in England in 1819 after many years of brilliant service as one of the directors of the East India Company.

Madhu Das's Gardens, the head-quarters first of Warren Hastings, and afterwards of the ex-Nawab Wazir Ali, in those stirring times, is an old pleasure-ground of the Mogul period, laid out with stone water-channels for irrigation and a square platform with a fountain in the centre. For the accommodation of the owner and his zenana there were airy pavilions in the centre of the four walls which surrounded it. The gardens are now in native hands, the water-channels are dried up, and the quarters are seldom occupied.

Except by an occasional riot between low-class Hindus and Muhammadans, such as has been described in the last chapter, and some trouble with a native regiment in the days of the Mutiny, Benares has not disturbed the *pax Britannica* since 1799.

From the Hindu point of view, the city has flourished exceedingly under British rule. Its temples and shrines have multiplied, and the strong arm of the law now prevents the desecration and destruction to which they were subject in Muhammadan times. The railways have largely increased the numbers of pilgrims who throng the ghâts and holy places, and have thus added to the offerings which enrich the Brahmin priesthood.

British influence has undoubtedly made for order, decency, cleanliness, and general sanitation in the city. But its effect on the foundations of Hindu beliefs is not very evident in Benares, the Rome of Hinduism, unless the spirit of exclusiveness which has sprung up of late years should be regarded as a sign of the Brahmins' alarm at the increasing influence of Christianity. When Sherring wrote his *Sacred City of the Hindus*, in the middle of the last century, he was allowed access to the most sacred places, which are now entirely closed to Europeans, even to the few who claim admission within the pale of the Hindu religion.

Benares has not ceased to be one of the great centres of the intellectual life of India, held in love and veneration by all Hindus; but the orthodox Brahmin looks askance at the efforts of Hindu propagandists, like Swami Vivekananda, who would strengthen resistance to outside influences by enlarging the borders of Hinduism.

The Hindu monasteries of Benares are still resorted to by students from all parts of India, for the education imparted by Brahmin Pandits, totally ignorant of modern research, and regarding as worthless all knowledge not contained in Hindu sacred literature. On the other hand, there is the extraordinary spectacle of a college for Hindus, supported both by Indians and Europeans, with English men and women expounding Hindu philosophy and religion to Hindus, and seeking to re-state the ancient Vedic wisdom on a basis of modern science.

Whether the Hindu Central College at Benares will survive the remarkable personality of its leading spirit, Mrs. Besant, may well be questioned, but there is no doubt that Hinduism will continue to be profoundly modified by the inflow of Western ideas. There can be no greater mistake than to consider Hinduism as so many immutable customs and forms of ritual and belief, which may be uprooted, but cannot be trained or adapted.

Just as thousands of years ago the Vedic Rishis, Vasishtha and Vishwamitra, represented two opposite schools, one of rigid orthodoxy and exclusiveness, the other of tolerance and progressive thought, so to-day there is, on the one side, the Brahmin of the old school, jealous of his social privileges, and guarding the ancient forms of his religion from the taint of innovation; and, on the other side, the Hindu who seeks to adjust the canons of his faith to social changes and the progress of human knowledge.

The strength of Hinduism has always lain, not in its exclusiveness, but in its extraordinary power of adaptation and assimilation. It is waste of energy for Christians to inveigh merely against Hindu superstition, idolatry, and caste. It is rather by sympathetic study of Hinduism in all its aspects that we shall learn to reach the hearts of the people, as our great Teacher did on the shores of Galilee.